THINGS MY DADDY USED TO SAY

By

G. E. Kruckeberg

ISBN: 1-4107-9814-3 (e-book)
ISBN: 1-4107-9813-5 (Paperback)

This book is printed on acid free paper.

1stBooks – rev. 09/18/03

This book is dedicated to my three sons,
Ed, Mark, and John

TABLE OF CONTENTS

FORWARD

The word "Daddy" evokes different memories and different emotions from different people. For some of us, Daddy was the guy we never knew. He was the man we missed as we were growing up – the man we lay awake at night wondering about – the man whose face and guidance and strength we looked for in grandfathers and uncles and in any man who would pay us the least bit of attention. For others of us, perhaps even less fortunate, Daddy was the man who was never there, even when he was.

But for most of us, Daddy was a cross between God and Santa Claus, and he is the one man we shall always remember with the fierce and uncompromising adoration of childhood.

When you were very young, your father was a force bigger than life itself. He was a giant who walked through your world with a will of his own, free to cuddle or to scold or to spank, seemingly at his whim, and usually without much interference from Mama.

Then, as you grew older, the god became a man, but still a man of heroic proportions. Your Daddy will always be the strong, perpetually young man who set you atop your first horse, or the man who, over your mother's objections, bought you your first pocket knife and your first pair of roller skates and your first gun. He was the man who was there when you killed your first rabbit and your first deer – the man who taught you how to catch bass and ride a bicycle and whistle through your teeth. He was the man who always had time for you when you were growing up – the man you could always go to when you needed to talk things out, and the man you could always depend on for both good advice and confidentiality.

And when you finally become an adult in your own right, you still think of your Daddy as someone just a little lower than the immortals. You will always be proud of him, and – even after he's gone – you'll still want to make him proud of you. I guess everyone, at some time in their life, has thought their Daddy was the greatest man who ever lived. I still do.

I remember my Daddy as a big man. He stood six-foot-two with his boots off. And yet, he had an immense quietness about him that belied his strength, as though the harshness of the land had softened him even as it had softened his faded jeans and the dust-colored cowhide boots he always wore. Beneath that softness, however, lay a resolve as hard and as sharp as a steel spur. I have seen those same big, brown hands tenderly brush the fevered brow of a sick child and kill a snake, and I have watched those same crinkly, blue eyes fill with tears at the sight of a sunset and stare another man down in a bar.

My Daddy never went to college. He never made a lot of money or a big name for himself. He lived most of his life in the town where he was born. Yet despite his lack of sophistication, he was one of the wisest men I have ever known. He wasn't a saint – nor did he ever claim to be one – but he was a man, and for me he embodied everything that that word stands for. His was a philosophy born not of otherworldliness but of day-to-day necessity – a philosophy that valued effort above perfection and honor above survival. It is a philosophy that has stood me in good stead, and I hope that with the reading of this book, it will do the same for you.

THINGS MY DADDY USED TO SAY

HOW TO USE THIS BOOK

One of the most revealing bits of wisdom I picked up in the navy was the old adage: "You can say anything you want to an officer as long as you say 'Sir.'" The difference between saying, for example, "You're out of your !@#$%&* mind," and "You're out of your !@#$%&* mind, Sir," should be obvious even to those who might not enjoy the advantage of having served time in the military.

I have found, in a similar manner, that prefacing almost any statement, no matter how derogatory, with the phrase "my Daddy used to say" has the same disarming effect. Consider, for example, the difference between saying, "Your problem is your ambitions exceed your abilities," and saying something along the line of: "My Daddy used to say: 'Happiness is mostly a matter of matching abilities and ambitions.'" The first statement is a personal affront, requiring immediate satisfaction and demanding future retaliation. The second, however, is a totally impersonal observation. It doesn't even contain the word "you." Nor does it place embarrassing emphasis on the subject of ambition, but purports instead to address the neutral subject of happiness. Furthermore, whatever the listener may think of this advice, you've already disclaimed any personal responsibility for it by making it very clear up front that this is not your observation at all, but that of your father.

Similarly, I can say, "Only a fool would let a man lie to him," or I can say, "My Daddy always said: 'You can't lie to a man that's not a fool.'" In the first case, I've told the man point blank that he's a fool; in the second case, I've put him on the other side of the equation – and allowed him to save face. In either case, I have made my point.

Most of the aphorisms in this book are worded with the above in mind, and are categorized for convenience under fifty-eight alphabetically arranged headings, from ADMIRATION to WORRY, making it easy for the aspiring gamesman to find and memorize the gems of wisdom contained herein and to apply them in context.

In the unlikely event you can't find what you want between these covers, take the trouble to read over what you've just read, and you'll find I've given you the formula for making up your own *bon mots*. (Well, maybe not quite *all* of the formula.)

In any case, good hunting.

ADMIRATION

Carlyle said, "No nobler feeling than that of admiration for one higher than himself dwells in the breast of man." Now, I can tell you with some certainty that my Daddy never read a whole lot of Carlyle, but he did seem to echo that sentiment (and to comment, incidentally, on the nature of nobility) when he said, "Admiration's not a normal human response, because it assumes that somebody is better at something than you are."

By his own measure, my Daddy was an eminently normal human being – a man untainted by the artificiality of noble feelings. While there were a great many people that he befriended during his lifetime, there were but few that my Daddy honestly admired. "Admiration," he was fond of saying, "is what you get from reading something about a man you don't know that was written about him by some press agent who didn't know him either."

I should like to think that Daddy's seeming cynicism was due to an uncommon ability to look behind the masks that people hide behind and to see the secret motives and fears and desires that drive them. I suspect, however, that the real reason for his aplomb was the conviction that all men are pretty much the same. "There are no heroes," he once told me. "A hero is just somebody that's got a dirtier job than most other folks."

But although Daddy's realism may have caused him to run short of heroes, that is one debility that I did not inherit – mainly because I had him.

A man can't admire what he can't respect.

3

You admire people not for what they did, but for what you think they're going to do.

People stumble mostly from looking up.

Nobody admires admiration except the admired.

A man admires folks that share his prejudices.

Don't admire a man for being on time. It probably just means he didn't have anything better to do.

A man ought to work harder to gain folk's respect than he does to gain their admiration.

Few men are admired by their friends, fewer still by their wives, and almost none by their kids.

Admiration, unlike charity, does not begin at home.

You can't help admiring a man who risks everything – even if he wins.

Most folks would rather be admired than loved – because admirers are a whole lot more tolerant than lovers.

We love what submits to us, and we admire what makes us submit.

A man admires what he doesn't have.

Admiration of others is founded on self-pity.

The only man that's really worthy of your admiration is the man that's wearing your britches.

Admiration is always cheaper than aspiration.

The need for admiration is the father of excellence.

The most admired things are usually the most useless.

Admiration of other folks turns their heads to gold – and our feet to clay.

Fools admire what men of sense reprove.

Most folks admire virtue more through folly than through accord.

Admiration is the illegitimate son of ambition.

Admire a man for what he is, not for what he's got.

Most folks will admire a man for being dishonest as long as he does it with style.

A lot of what folks call admiration is really a cover-up for jealousy.

Most men would rather be envied than pitied.

Flattery is the food of fools.

Flattery will get you everywhere – except ahead.

Admiration is often an end in itself, but flattery is always a means.

The only difference between a flatterer and a liar is that a flatterer is talking about you.

The difference between praise and flattery is the difference between good intentions and bad inventions.

Flattery is the fuel of vanity.

Flatterers and masochists most generally get what they ask for.

Your most dangerous flatterer is you.

Listen to your flatterers; the things that they tell you you're best at are usually the things that you need to work on the hardest.

The more dishonest the flattery, the more effective it usually is.

People admire honesty, as long as you don't tell them the truth.

It's a whole lot easier to admire a man's deeds than it is to admire the man.

I never met a man I truly admired – or a woman I didn't.

ADVICE

It was the middle of August, and the noonday sun made everything on the other side of the smoke stained windows stand out in almost colorless bas-relief, like a scene illuminated by a flashbulb that had forgotten to go out. Wrapped in the cool shadows of the dark-paneled bar room and lulled by the buzz of male voices and the smell of tobacco smoke and the electric hum of the overhead fans, I sucked the ice from my already finished root beer and listened to a thin, rather intent young man telling my father a tale that involved a woman and some alleged improprieties on her part, the import of which I did not, at the time, fully comprehend.

"Well, Ed," he said at last, "what do you think?"

"I think," Daddy said slowly, "that priests are paid to give advice and that they don't need competition from me."

That statement pretty much summed up Daddy's feelings on the subject of advice. It was a thing not to be sought, taken lightly, or given freely. "Every man has got to stand on his own two feet," he used to say, "which isn't too hard as long as he doesn't try to stand on somebody else's."

Some of the other things Daddy had to say on the subject are listed below – but with this disclaimer: they represent only instances of my Daddy's insights into human nature and are in no way offered as advice.

The best advice you can give somebody is to not give advice to anybody.

Never give people advice. Either they will take it and blame you for being wrong, or they won't take it and blame you for being right.

Advice is mostly criticism masquerading as Christian charity.

Advice doesn't cost you anything – as long as you don't take it.

Advice is mostly a matter of give and take. Good advice is what I give and bad advice is what I usually take.

Good men generally give bad advice.

The only good advice is mine.

The reason young folks don't follow your advice is that they are too busy following your example.

Advice is about the only thing a man ought to feel guilty about sharing with others.

A desperate man grasps at advice for the same reason a drowning man grasps at straws, and usually with the same effect.

About the only thing folks won't blame you for keeping to yourself is advice.

Most folks that ask for your advice really want your pity.

Advice is something a man gets from friends and enemies with equal malice.

Most folks will take anything that's free except responsibility and good advice.

There's no such thing as unpretentious advice.

If you're really concerned about me, don't give me advice – give me money.

Never give a man advice in love – or in any other kind of gambling.

There are two things a wise man never does to a woman: try to give her advice and refuse to take it from her.

The man that keeps his own counsel will never have to hire himself one.

If you have got to advise somebody, advise them to do what they have already decided to do.

Your money and your advice are two things best kept to yourself.

A man that offers you advice is usually more interested in impressing you than he is in helping you.

The less you know about something, the easier it is to give advice about it.

If more folks took their own advice, they wouldn't be so danged anxious to give it.

Your own advice is always cheaper.

It's always safer to advise folks what *not* to do.

Advice is as hard to take as castor oil – and a lot of it seems to have about the same effect.

Never trust a woman's advice, and never trust a woman that asks for yours.

The only man likely to profit from good advice is the man that didn't take it.

It'll usually cost you less to take a man's wallet than it will to take his advice.

Today's advice is tomorrow's "I told you so."

If people who try to give you advice really knew what they were talking about, they'd be charging you for it.

Expert is spelled e-x p-o-s-t f-a-c-t-o.

The more a man pays for advice, the more likely he is to take it.

Never give advice to a man that's bigger than you are.

Advice is like a woman: it's usually a whole lot easier to take than it is to live with.

Never take advice from a woman you don't intend to keep.

That's the best advice I've had since my wife told me to marry her.

If you swallow the advice folks give you, it most generally turns into the same thing everything else you swallow turns into.

AMBITION

My Daddy was an ambitious man, but unlike Caesar, his ambitions were not for himself. They were mostly for my brother and me. He seemed to see in us a second chance to realize the frustrated ambitions of his own youth, and he was always eager to assist us in whatever endeavor we might undertake.

But his ambitions encompassed a wider circle than just the immediate family. While his first concern was always for the welfare of Mama and my brother and me, I have never known him to refuse any reasonable request for assistance from anyone. I've seen him loan money to people to pay debts or rent or doctor bills knowing full well he would never be repaid, and I've seen him in his Sunday clothes helping a neighbor round up his runaway pigs.

Nor was his charity confined to friends and acquaintances. Fortunate was the stranger stuck in a mud hole or sweating under the hood of a recalcitrant vehicle whom my Daddy happened upon. Quite simply, my Daddy was a good Samaritan, and if he had any great ambition in life it was just to help as many people as possible as much as he could.

It is my sincere belief that that ambition is one that we all might emulate to our advantages.

Things are never so bad that they couldn't be better.

Wanting to take what somebody else has got is greed; wanting to *make* what *nobody* else has got is ambition.

Ambition never looks back.

Folks will aspire to whatever they think other folks will believe, and they will generally believe whatever they think other folks will aspire to.

Ambition is a mental disease that men get from their wives.

There are three things that no man can ever satisfy: women, tax collectors, and ambition.

Frustration is ambition without ability.

Ambition is always strongest in the inexperienced.

Ambition is that still, small voice that keeps telling you you're wasting your time where you are and you ought to be working your buns off to get into a position where you can waste even more time.

A man's future is in his ambitions.

Always be suspicious of a man that's ambitious.

Satisfaction and ambition are mortal enemies.

Ambition is like a beautiful woman: it promises more than it can deliver and demands more than most men are willing to give.

We are seldom given what we want; but we're always given what we need to *make* what we want.

Ambition's like the mumps: once you've had it and got over it, you'll never get it again.

If a man's ambitious, he doesn't have to be real smart; and if he's real smart, he won't be ambitious.

Ambition is the father of indolence.

A man can't be more than what he aspires to be – and he'll never be any less.

Ambition is what makes a man search out all of the latest and most modern methods and technology so he can use them to make enough money to decorate his house with stuff his grandmother would've thrown away.

Ambition isn't always bad – sometimes it's the only thing that keeps a man from dying of boredom.

A man can't fail if he's not ambitious.

If you can't figure out which way to go, it could be 'cause you don't know where you want to be.

A man that chokes his ambition is strangling his future.

Ambition is what separates the men from the joys.

Distrust comes of ambition and conceit.

Ambition's a lot like lust: it wears a man down until he can't enjoy what he wants when he gets it.

There are only two things in the world can make a free man into a slave: love and ambition.

A man pays his debts to feed his pride, but he borrows to feed his ambition.

Ambition makes a whole lot more debtors than poverty.

Ambitious people are always too busy working to hear opportunity when it knocks.

A problem is an opportunity you didn't take.

My only ambition is fishin'.

Ambition is kinder than age – it makes a man ugly only on the inside.

Trusting an ambitious man with a secret is like trusting a pimp with your daughter.

Ambition is the fear of being poor.

Lucifer's downfall wasn't ambition – it was losing.

Ambition's only bad if you can't afford it.

A man without ambition is either a bum or a saint.

Laziness is the father of ambition.

Most of the great inventions in history were made by lazy people.

The one thing that humans do that the other animals don't do is aspire.

ANGER

Daddy had just parked in front of the hardware store on Broadway, although our destination was Meyer's Drug Store, a half block down the street. It was late July, and as I jumped down from the cab of the truck, the sudden sting of hot concrete on the bottoms of my bare feet elicited a string of angry and profane words, which I regretted even as I was skipping over to the cooler pavement under the big, red awning of the hardware store.

I could see from the look on Daddy's face that I was in for a stern reprimand. Before he could say anything, however, the front door of the hardware store flew open and the young man who clerked there charged out and accosted Daddy regarding an alleged discrepancy in his monthly billing.

Daddy managed to persuade the intense young man that he had merely paid the bill as presented to him and that if there were a discrepancy, he would be glad to make it right. The three of us, led by the clerk strutting like a little drum major, marched into the store and down the dingy aisles through the smells of oiled wood and leather and dusty steel and brass to the cluttered little office at the back of the store. The discrepancy – which was slight – turned out to be the fault entirely of the clerk. Daddy just pulled his concave wallet from his left hip pocket and, without saying a word, peeled out the number of sweat-stained greenbacks required to settle the account.

When we walked back out into the sunlight, I said, "Why was he so mad?"

"Well," Daddy answered, "I believe he was scared."

"Scared?" I said. "Scared of what?"

"I don't know," Daddy shrugged. "'Maybe getting fired or catching hell from his boss – or more likely catching hell from his boss's daughter,

15

who happens to be his wife." Daddy reached down and tousled my hair with his big hand as we walked on down the street to the drug store. "Y'know," he said after a few seconds, "I reckon maybe in most cases, 'anger' starts with a 'D'."

I should like to think this insight sank immediately into my fertile brain and took root. The truth, however, is that only after years of exposure to human nature did the import of my father's words become obvious to me. And frankly, that irritates me. But then, as Daddy always said, "The one thing that'll get people mad quicker than anything else is their own ignorance."

When a man loses his temper, he loses the only thing he's got going for him – the general appearance of sanity.

The hardest thing in the world to recover is a lost temper.

Where passion rules, reason abdicates.

The man that loses his temper loses the argument.

Pride is the fuel of anger.

A man doesn't waste his anger on somebody he doesn't like.

Anger is the father of regret.

The things a man is likely to get mad about are usually things he's already lost – or things he never did have in the first place.

Be slow to anger and quick to retaliate.

He that is slow to anger is quick to be taken advantage of.

A man that gets mad at a dumb animal is.

Only a coward would cuss something that can't cuss him back.

Apology is a better cure for embarrassment than anger.

Getting mad as a hornet about something means getting mad enough to die for it.

One thing that really ticks me off is folks always getting ticked off about things.

Don't get mad. Get even – tempered.

Losing your temper is like losing your virtue – every time you do it, it gets easier.

Sometimes a man's got to chose between losing his temper and losing.

A man that keeps losing his cool usually ends up in the cooler.

Mad and angry may not mean the same thing, but they sure do look a lot alike.

The best cure for getting mad is a good dose of sanity.

Anger is often the remembrance of past injustices.

Wrath and righteousness are not bounded by reason.

Anger, fear, and smallpox have one thing in common: they're all contagious.

"Vengeance is mine," saith the mob.

Revenge is unnatural in nature and inhuman in humans.

Revenge is the last resort of the incompetent.

Folks that worry too much about getting even aren't worrying enough about getting ahead.

Anger is a bitter wine, and its vinegar is vengeance.

If all a man's trying to do is get even, he's dang sure going to fall behind.

A man can't lose his temper and keep his self-respect.

Most of the things that folks get mad about are things that nobody else is even aware of.

Anger is a poor cure for inferiority – but it's a dang sure sign of it.

A man's got to be angry with himself before he can get angry with other folks.

'Best way to deal with a man with a chip on his shoulder is as little as possible.

Anger is the highest form of egotism – and the lowest form of masochism.

Nobody ever won a confrontation.

ATTITUDE

"I don't like your attitude," I can remember my Daddy saying. In fact, of all the things my Daddy said, I remember that admonition most vividly, probably because it was most often directed at me, and because Daddy could say it in a way that would send a chill up a boy's spine – or a man's.

Attitude, I learned quite early in life, was a very important commodity to my Daddy. He considered it to be a man's greatest asset – or his greatest liability – and a bad one was a thing that he could not abide. To Daddy, a bad attitude was the harbinger of failure, and he was particularly impatient with anyone whom he suspected of actually nurturing one. I remember the time Daddy was berating me about what he perceived to be a lack of proper diligence and application in the conduct of my schoolwork. When I started to respond with a long list of excuses, Daddy held up his hand. "Boy, I don't want to hear about your problems," he said. "Problems are like good looks – only a damn fool thinks he's the only one that's got any."

A goodly part of my Daddy's educational efforts consisted of such admonitions, and a lot of what he said had to do with attitude. His approach to making men out of boys was more verbal than physical – he seemed to believe that a well-turned, even humorous phrase would stick to a boy's ribs far longer than a whipping with a hickory switch. He was right, and lest the rich legacy of his attempt be lost forever to posterity, I've endeavored to set down here as much of it as I can remember.

19

A man's nothing but an attitude wearing a hat.

The only thing most folks see is your attitude.

The best way to keep smiling is to start.

Personality is just a big word for attitude.

A man's attitude depends a lot on how much money he's got in his pocket.

The cheapest facelift you can get is a smile.

The first mark of inferiority is the belief that you're better than anybody else.

A man's attitude tends to get better the less options he's got.

Attitude can make an opportunity out of a problem – or a problem out of an opportunity.

You can pretty much tell a man's attitude by how clean his boots are.

Optimism is an attitude of both geniuses and fools.

The right attitude and a dime'll get you a good cup of coffee. A dime'll get you just a cup of coffee.

A man can borrow trouble all day long and not have any -but if he tries to lend it, he gets it back with interest.

Two things look bigger than they really are: anticipated trouble and expected pleasure.

Winter comes before Spring – or after it, depending on your attitude.

Pride cometh before a brawl.

Attitude can make a gentleman out of a bum, but it most generally works the other way around.

A bad attitude is like a toothache: it only hurts the guy that has got it.

Bad luck is a sure sign of a bad attitude.

Only God and fools take irreversible positions. The difference is that God doesn't have a family to feed.

A man's attitude is his own business. And if he's smart, he'll make it his only business.

All things come to those who love to bitch.

Patience may be a virtue – it just doesn't happen to be one of mine.

Most folks would rather change their politics than their attitude.

The only effective attitude modifier I know of is a three foot length of two-by-four.

The beginning of wisdom is the realization that nobody owes you a danged thing.

Problem is opportunity spelled backwards.

If you were really trying to fix the problem, you wouldn't have the *time* to bitch about it.

Those who do excel; those who don't complain.

A man's philosophy is a feature of his profession.

Self-confidence is a symptom of success.

BEING A MAN

"Live your life in such a way that you never have to apologize to anybody."

That maxim – the categorical imperative of the Southern gentleman – was the rule by which my Daddy lived. It was his modus operandi, and I have tried, with some success, to make it mine.

I think it is a good rule – as good a rule for guiding a man's life as it is for measuring it – and I would recommend it to all men everywhere who have a desire to improve themselves. I believe that the man who lives by those words will always walk proud. He will not be dismayed by the trappings of power and authority. Nor will he ever know fear and indecision, for his way and his conscience will always be clear. Such a man can well afford to accommodate the weaknesses of others, for his strength far surpasses his own needs, and he will never want for the love of faithful friends.

My Daddy lived by those words. To him, they were what being a man is all about. Of course, ha had a lot of other things to say about being a man – sparkling little *bon mots* that he sprinkled along the paths of my youth, subtly candy-coated with the disarming humor with which he viewed all of life. I have set down here a few examples of that legacy, but I should like to caution the reader against interpreting them as directions for being a man. They are more on the order of tongue-in-cheek comments on the state of being a man, valuable at most as small signposts along the road to masculinity. But then, that's all my Daddy ever meant them to be. Most of what he taught me about being a man he taught me by example.

'Ain't but two things in this world a man can count on: himself and his fingers.

A man is never less than what he is, and he'll never be more than what he wants to be.

A man has got to stand for something, even if it's something stupid.

A man always does what he wants to do, but what a man wants to do is always what's right.

A man is what he walks like.

You've got to be a man to know what one is.

If a man's got self-respect, he'll always have the respect of at least one man.

What a man is supposed to be depends a whole lot on who it is that's doing the supposing.

Being a man means you never stop learning how.

"Fix" is what a man is expected to do; it's not something he's supposed to get himself into.

A man's faith has got to be in himself. 'Course God can help out all He wants to.

A man is what he does, and nobody really cares much about why he did it.

The only proper measure of a philosophy is the kind of men it makes.

A nice man is not the same thing as a good man.

It may be true that a man is born to die, but it's what he does in between that counts.

In spite of all our modern technology, there is still one thing that every man has got to make for himself: opportunity.

You can't be a man without being a part of mankind.

A man owes his accomplishments to the men who came before him, and he owes the fruits of his accomplishments to the men who come after him.

You can always judge a man by his dreams.

Being a man may not always be easy, but it sure as hell can be fun sometimes.

Trouble is like a mirror – it shows you what kind of man you are.

Never trust a gun – or a man – without proof marks.

A man can be whatever he wants to be, but he usually ends up being whatever his wife wants him to be.

A man alone is just a man, but two men together are boys.

Bounders and gentlemen put their pants on the same way – the difference is in how they take a woman's off.

The toughest man you will ever have to fight is yourself.

The best gift a man can give to his son is a good example.

If a man doesn't take the example of others, he's dang sure going to be used as an example *to* others.

Decide what you want and go after it. Most folks'll get out of the way of anyone who knows where he's going.

A thing worth doing is a thing worth doing again.

You're better off being sorry for *doing* something than for *not* doing it.

A man that knows what he's doing is either a genius or a dang good liar.

No man is an island, but I have met quite a few that were atolls.

Being wrong is a lot easier than being right because there are more ways of doing it.

There is no substitute for knowing what the hell you're doing.

A man's gotta rue what a man's gotta rue.

A real man would rather be right than be president, but most of us have found that both aspirations exceed our capabilities.

A man has got to be for himself, because if he's not, he sure as shootin' won't get anybody else to be.

Shame is the loss of self-respect, not the respect of others.

A brave man walks away from a fight; a coward runs.

A man doesn't argue unless he thinks he's right.

A man says what he thinks – not what he wants other folks to think.

A man may be smarter'n a horse, but the horse has got the man feeding him.

Sons are cast not in the molds of their fathers but in the molds of their father's expectations.

A man's a lot like bamboo: as soon as he shows you his foliage, he shows you where his roots are.

Luck is a thing that a man has got to work hard at.

You're not committed until you do something.

There are times when a man's got to be difficult – the times when he's right.

A man can live only one day at a time, but he's got to make sure it's today.

BUSINESS

My Daddy wasn't much of a businessman, but it wasn't because he didn't try. In fact he was always, it seemed, trying something – from playing guitar to manufacturing battery powered electric cattle prods. Some things he made money at and some things he never got off the ground, but Daddy never did believe in keeping score. "Business," he used to say, "is kind of a game. It's not the money you enjoy so much as it is just the fun of playing." Like any other game my Daddy played, he played hard and he played to win. But he wouldn't cheat. I guess maybe that's why he never did get rich.

Daddy wasn't one to let disappointment cloud his perception, however, and win lose or draw, he always came away a little bit smarter. Some of what he'd learned he imparted to me as I was growing up, in the hope, I suppose, that I might be more successful than he had been.

But I guess business was never meant to be my vocation. Or maybe I was always too busy trying to emulate my father's success in those areas of life that I consider – and that I believe he considered as well – to be more important.

In any case, what I can remember of what he told me I have set down for the edification of those of you who might be able to understand it.

Saving money is a poor substitute for making it.

Spend money to save money; borrow money to make money.

If you borrow like a Democrat, you've got to spend like a Republican.

A bank is an institution that borrows money for an obscene pittance and loans it for an obscene profit.

Profit is the cost of capital.

Waste makes haste.

Business is ten percent knowing what you're doing and ninety percent knowing who you're doing it to.

Assuming is done mostly in retrospect.

In business, it's not so much who you know; it's how much you got on 'em.

A business organization is not a democracy – it's a feudal society, and it operates by fealty and noblesse oblige.

The mass of men lead lives of fiat dedication.

When you understand the rat race, it tends to make you more of an observer than a participant.

Never work two Saturdays in a row, because when you don't come in on the third Saturday, your boss will think that *you* are cheating *him*.

The man that knows how will always have a job, and the man that knows who will always be his boss.

'Fellow that's working on a few things is an entrepreneur, but the fellow that's got a few things working for him is a pimp.

A thing is worth only what you can sell it for.

A man that tries to pick himself up by his boot straps ends up picking himself up off his ass.

If it sounds too good to be true, you haven't read all the fine print.

Look before you lease.

If you've got to keep reminding yourself to do something, it's probably something you shouldn't be doing.

When you're damned if you do and damned if you don't, delegate.

Look out for people who "address" problems; address means to put somebody else's name on it.

If you're not sure, guess high.

Low budgets breed low profits.

Speed won't help if you're going the wrong way.

If at first you don't succeed, revise the plan.

Memos are like women's bathing suits: their purpose is to cover up just enough so that nobody gets too excited.

There are only two reasons a man would write a memo: either he's trying to show himself off or he's a mute.

The two greatest time saving devices in the world are the telephone and the wastebasket – the first keeps you from wasting your time writing memos and the second keeps you from wasting your time reading them.

If a man takes the time to write a memo about it, it's usually too late to do anything about it.

People who write memos are usually looking for someone to tell them what to do, and the people who answer memos usually don't know.

Any meeting between more than two people is a waste of time.

Things get done one on one.

The main reason for business meetings seems to be to give people something to write reports about.

G. E. Kruckeberg

The average business meeting costs a company $250 per hour per attendee: the $30 in salary and benefits the guy's being paid, the $20 he could have made for the company if he hadn't been in a meeting, and $200 because his staff is goofing off while he's in the meeting.

Useful work output is inversely proportional to the amount of time spent talking about it.

Meetings are like rabbits: you put two of 'em together and before you know it you got a whole string of the dang things.

The second time I call somebody and his secretary tells me he's in a meeting, I ask to talk to somebody else. I figure anybody that spends all their time in meetings doesn't know what's going on anyhow.

The best time to solve a problem is before it becomes one.

The cheapest and most productive capital we have is people's minds.

The idea is not to solve problems, but to train your people not to make 'em.

It always costs more to fix a problem than it does to just go ahead and prevent it.

Most problems are caused by somebody taking themselves too seriously.

The higher a man gets in a company, the more money he gets – and the less money he makes.

The difference between RUN a company and RUIN a company is just one letter – I.

Prices are like women's panties: 'fellow that really knows what he's doing can always get them down.

Nobody cares what you did if you can't sell it.

In business, it's not so much what you say – it's what other folks hear.

If you don't know what you're talking about, don't.

If you got the only stud horse in the county, you got a monopoly, if there're eight or ten others around just as good, you gotta advertise.

Advertising enhances your competition – as long as they're not advertising too.

Economists are wasting their time arguing demand side and supply side. What drives the economy is the advertising side.

Advertising increases price as well as demand, so the trick is to never buy anything that's advertised and advertise the hell out of whatever it is you're selling.

If you re-design your product so it won't last as long, people will buy more – from your competitors.

The quickest way to lose a friend is to go into business with him.

Every great week in history has begun with a Monday.

Any day that begins with an "F" is a good day.

If your days start looking better from the back end than they do from the front end, you're probably in the wrong job.

When prices go up, quality goes down.

When you're in business, you find yourself spending a lot of time training your competition's future employees.

Loyalty is only me deep.

Acquisition is going into debt to buy something that's producing so poorly that the current owners want to sell it.

The business you're in is not determined by the market you serve but by the service you market.

JIT stands for "Just Inventory it There."

If you got a choice between two evils, pick the one that's more profitable.

When you're in business, you're like a log in a stream: you've got to keep moving ahead just to stay even.

There are three types of business meetings: anorexic, nauseating, and emetic.

A business is like a fishing expedition. The Production Department runs the boat, the Engineering Department cuts bait, and the Accounting Department cleans the fish. But they're all working for the Sales Department, 'cause they're the fishermen.

CAUTION

When I was in college, I became imbued for a time with the liberal tenets of the civil rights movement. Daddy, understandably, viewed this segment of my education with some misgivings. It wasn't that he disagreed with the objectives of the movement; he just couldn't agree with the methods. It was impossible for him to understand how restricting the rights of one group could enhance those of another, or how civil disobedience could possibly contribute to the civil rights of anyone – with the obvious exception of anarchists.

He was, however, surprisingly tolerant of my views – except on this last point. On the one occasion that I suggested the possibility of my actually taking part in a demonstration, he balked. "Boy, let me tell you something," he said. "It is true that the First Amendment gives you the right to go around saying any damn-fool thing you want. But the Second Amendment tells you that only a damn fool would."

Three months later, a little college in Kent, Ohio became, for a brief period, the most famous university in the world.

Things are never so good that they couldn't be worse.

Never try something you haven't seen somebody else do.

An ill wind is the one you threw caution to.

G. E. Kruckeberg

No matter how many times you've shaved, you can still cut yourself.

Caution is the crown of courage.

Much ado is never about nothing.

Showing your wisdom around some folks can be more dangerous than showing your ignorance.

If you're not smart, you gotta be careful.

Fishers of men always bait their hooks with false hope.

The two most frightening words in the English language are "trust me."

Trust not, want not.

If you're not gonna shoot, don't draw.

Don't wear your spurs when you're making love.

A smart man'll learn caution from other folks' mistakes.

Caution is the tempering of desire with fear.

More hopes have been dashed by caution than by audacity.

If you want something done right, do it when you're sober.

'Fellow that's always telling you how great you are is either a fool or he's after something you got.

Don't let a sleeping lie dog you.

A man that's always baiting folks is liable to get chopped up for bait someday.

Testing a man's patience is like testing his home made whiskey: if he fails the test, you're the one that's in trouble.

If it sounds too good to be true, bet the ranch on it. In this State we got a homestead exemption.

The more you keep your mouth shut, the harder it is to put your foot in it.

Faint heart never won fair.

Never trust a woman that swears – or a man that doesn't.

Always be friendly to everybody, but never trust a stranger.

Never play poker with strangers.

I don't like card sharks, but I do enjoy playing with folks who think they are.

There's nothing more dangerous than a man that's scared.

Whenever somebody tells me I've got just two choices, I know they're trying to push me into one of theirs.

Don't stand downwind of a man that chews tobacco.

Just because cowards are cautious doesn't mean every cautious man is a coward.

If you bury the hatchet, just don't forget where.

Caution is a response to danger; panic is a response to fear.

The difference between caution and cowardice is the difference between walking and running.

'Man that runs is either a coward or a fool, depending on which way he's running.

Caution is the bitter part of valor.

Caution is a thing that a man has got to learn, but it's a thing he won't have long to regret if he doesn't.

A cautious man is a man that's still around.

If the grass were really greener on the other side, the fence would be higher.

He who hesitates is usually glad later that he did.

COMMON SENSE

"Common sense," Daddy used to say, "is the human species most uncommon attribute." Nor was my Daddy an idle critic on the subject. He had been born or blessed with a great deal of that rarest of commodities – although he preferred to call it "horse sense" – and he seemed to derive no little satisfaction from calling other people's attention to that fact.

I remember back in the "affirmative action" era, when an undernourished young woman, wearing oversized horn rim glasses and a dress that had gone out of style eight years earlier, accused Daddy of discrimination.

Daddy pushed his hat back, gave her a big smile, and said, "Why, thank you, ma'am."

The lipless mouth went slack and the eyes behind the thick lenses seemed to get even bigger. "Thank you?" she gasped. "What do you mean 'thank you'?"

"Honey," he said, "in these parts folks admire discrimination. It's the only thing that keeps a man from polishing his boots with cow pies."

Some of the other things Daddy had to say about common sense are listed below. They are out of context, I'm afraid, since it would require far too much time and space to relate here the incident that elicited each comment. But then, as Daddy always said, "The nice thing about common sense is that it tends to work in any situation."

Common sense will tell you what you usually don't want to hear.

A lot of folks think they have common sense when all they really have is common prejudices.

Common sense is what a man uses to tell the difference between sense and nonsense.

If it looks like horse manure and smells like horse manure, only a damn fool would taste it to see if it really is.

A smart man will kill a rattlesnake *before* it bites him.

If it works, let it.

Don't fix it if you didn't break it.

If you don't know what you're doing, don't.

Man that uses a little common sense won't use near so much Malox and Alka-Seltzer.

To everything there is a reason.

A sense of humor is common sense tempered with nonsense.

A genius is just somebody that's got more common sense than most folks.

One fact is worth a million opinions.

A man can believe the world is flat just as hard as he wants to, but it won't make it any less round.

Burning bridges won't do a whole lot of good if the enemy has got boats.

Don't buy time if you're not going to use it.

A penny saved is a penny taken out of circulation.

A dollar saved will be worth about 94 cents at the end of the first year.

To my knowledge, nobody in his right mind has ever accused a politician of being overly familiar with the basic precepts of common sense.

Early to bed and early to rise makes a man dull.

It may be a horse of a different color, but it still smells like a horse.

Common sense is mostly a lack of opinion.

It takes more than a map to get someplace – you've also got to have some idea of where you want to go.

It's kind of hard for folks to appreciate what they don't know.

Anybody can lead a horse to water, but it takes a hell of a man to drown him.

To most folks, common sense means the sense that's common among their acquaintances.

Wearing a yarmulke won't make you Jewish, but it sure will make folks think you are.

Common sense seems to be inversely proportional to uncommon intelligence.

Wisdom is knowledge and common sense put together.

Common sense is like wealth: most folks would be higher on it if they had more of it.

It's mostly wanting something that blinds a man to common sense.

Common sense seems to be most common among common people.

Common sense is like wine: a little bit may improve your wit, but too much can make you dull as a dunce.

Where I come from, common sense is called horse sense. Maybe that's because horses have got more of it than most people.

Too often, common sense is what's common on TV.

COMPARATIVES AND SUPERLATIVES

"Boy," I can still hear my Daddy saying, "you're about as bright as a glint in a redbug's eye." Whenever I heard that expression (and as I recall it was not all that infrequently) I was sure that Daddy was thoroughly exasperated with my performance – or lack of it. And although the words bring a smile to my lips today, they fell on the shoulders of my youth with far greater force than a string of obscenities would have.

But obscenity would have been out of character for my Daddy. You seldom heard him cuss – or more accurately, you seldom heard him cuss out of context. His abstinence wasn't so much due to an aversion to profanity as it was to a conviction that its continual use tended to detract from the richness and beauty of the language. To Daddy's way of thinking, "cold as hell" was not only a trite expression; it was contrary to popular legend concerning the climate of that area. But an expression like "cold as an old maid's feet," now, is far more accurate and a whole lot more interesting – and its use bespeaks a man of experience as well as verbal discretion.

While I doubt that Daddy ever felt a conscious need to enrich the language, his passion for originality did, at least within the circle of his acquaintances, often have that result. Nowhere was this more apparent than in some of his more colorful comparatives, a few of which I have set down here in the hope that the reader might find them valuable in spicing his own conversation.

Addictive as peanuts.

Aggressive as a tax collector.

Agile as a woman with a hornet in her drawers.

Ambitious as prohibition.

As bad as you can get without being arrested.

So bad if it got any worse it'd be better.

Belligerent as a castrated bull.

Belligerent as a non-combatant.

Best thing that's happened since repeal.

Better than sex and a whole lot cheaper.

Better than going to heaven, and you don't have to die first.

Biased as the stripes on a politician's tie.

Bigger'n Dolly Parton's bra.

Big as the Oklahoma sky.

Bigger than a preacher's ego.

Big as a young man's dreams.

Black as Mississippi bottom land.

Black as Texas crude.

Black as a union list.

Bleak as a Louisiana Republican's prospects.

Blind as a woman in love.

Blue as the air around Eddie Murphy's mouth.

Blue as a Texas Spring.

Boring as a "Leave It To Beaver" rerun.

Brave as a barking dog.

Broke as a politician's promise.

Harder to change than a Southern Democrat.

Cheaper than cold weather in January.

About as cheap as a free lunch.

Colder'n a dry ice enema.

Colder'n a jilted woman.

Cold enough to freeze a candle flame.

Cold as an ethnic joke.

So cold I was dang glad I wasn't a brass monkey.

Coming up faster'n gophers in a gullywashser.

Common as idiots in Washington.

About as common as an honest lawyer.

Cool as a mule's tool.

Crookeder'n Louisiana politics.

He's got a mind like a steel trap – dangerous.

Dangerous as a dull knife.

Dangerous as a 30-30 spitzer.

More dangerous than a sack of rattlesnakes.

Darker'n a Georgia swamp.

Dark as a prostitute's past.

Deader'n the Equal Rights Amendment.

Deaf as a kid watching TV.

Devious as the mother of an unmarried woman.

'Bout as diplomatic as Don Rickles – when he's drunk.

He's got about as much diplomacy as a hangman.

Dull as a Wednesday night sermon.

Dumb as a box of rocks.

Dumb enough to believe a TV advertisement.

About as easy as giving a tiger an enema.

About as exciting as a traffic jam.

Exciting as a woman's smile.

Almost as exciting as listening to corn grow.

Expensive as voting Democrat.

Faster'n a woman can say no.

As hard to find as a transvestite in a nudist colony.

Harder to find than a straw in a needle stack.

Flat as last night's beer.

So flat you can see the crown on a road a mile away.

As free as bad advice.

More fun than group sex.

Funny as a broken leg.

The greatest thing since edible panties.

A bigger grouser than a ten gauge Browning.

Gullible as a Cook County democrat.

Happy as a pig in a mudhole.

Healthy as a man with no insurance.

Higher'n a redneck on a Friday night.

As big a hit as the Edsel.

Honest as a politician in an election year.

I got so many honey-dos I feel like a melon patch.

Hotter'n a boot full of fire ants.

Indignant as an ex-smoker at a poker game.

Liberal as a newly elected Democrat.

Loose as an Exlax addict.

Looser'n an Arab coalition.

Nervous as a cat in a kennel.

Noiser'n a gaggle of geese.

Nutty as a squirrel.

If the best defense is a good offense, he's the most defensive man I ever met.

Open as a church.

persistent as kudzu.

Pious as a hypocrite.

About as popular as a Susan B. Anthony dollar.

Pretty as the south side of a woman going north.

So prejudiced he thinks NAACP stands for Negro Auxiliary of the American Communist Party.

Quick as a woman can change her mind.

Rare as an honest politician.

Talking to him's like dropping stones down a dry well.

Rougher'n a Mississippi grade crossing.

Sanctimonious as an ex-smoker.

Sexy as a castrated mule.

Sharp as a cow pie and twice as smart.

Shocked as the first time you heard your mother cuss.

So shy he thinks girl is a four-letter word.

Slow as a woman making up her mind.

Slower'n an ant swimming across a bucket of tar with an anvil tied to its tail.

Stickier'n Louisiana gumbo.

Straight as an Irishman heading for a bar.

Stubborn as an Arkansas Republican.

Sure as a Shodish follows a Cotton Eyed Joe.

Talking to him's like shaving with a dull razor.

Tighter'n a three dollar boot.

Thicker'n gulls around a shrimp boat.

They go together like Christmas and kids.

True as Dillinger's girl friend.

Ugly as gossip.

Uncomfortable as a sheep in wolf's clothing.

Virtuous as a reformed prostitute.

Wasteful as a coon in a corn patch.

Wide as the road to hell.

Wild as a preacher's son.

COMPETITION

I came home from school smarting from the somewhat less than gentlemanly comments the coach had made regarding my abilities – or lack thereof – in the game of football. My egocentric twelve year old brain found it impossible to comprehend how a man of such intimate acquaintance with the game should not be able to appreciate my unique talents, which I had taken the trouble to demonstrate on the practice field before his very eyes and the open mouths of my teammates.

As always, when confused by the seeming inconsistencies of the adult world, I went for counsel to my father. After listening patiently for several minutes, he said, "Boy, 'sounds to me like you were trying to run the whole show."

"Well," I said, from the depths of my infinite wisdom, "football *is* a competitive sport."

He looked at me for a long moment before he ran a hand over his stubbled chin and said, "Son, sports aren't competitive – men are competitive. Sports were invented to teach them how not to be."

I think that of all the things my Daddy said to me, that one insight into human nature has made more of an impression on my life than any other. But for the benefit of those who might not appreciate the universality of that insight, I have cited below a number of other things Daddy had to say about competition.

Life is competition.

G. E. Kruckeberg

Competition may not be fair, but it's the only game in town.

Folks cooperate only because they can compete better with help.

There's a word for folks that think competition is a bad thing: losers.

A man can't win if he doesn't have a little competition.

Losing wouldn't be so bad if you didn't have to compete to do it.

Competition is the only thing that'll keep a man honest.

The human spirit is the competitive spirit.

Don't play if you're not going to compete.

Competition is the lifeblood of commerce – it's the only thing that'll make a man mean enough to sell his soul for a profit.

Competition breeds competition.

A man's superiority or inferiority depends a whole lot on who he's with.

War and business and politics are just games that men invented because they couldn't find anybody but each other to compete with.

The meek already inherited the earth – and they lost it.

The only weakness is insecurity.

Never pit your strengths against their weaknesses; pit their weaknesses against your strengths.

Slow people don't get a lot – and what they do get, they get late.

Competition is a man's delight – and a woman's despair.

Competition is not made by men; men are made by competition.

Cooperation is the means; the end is competition.

48

In the game of life there are only two kinds of players: those who compete and those who lose.

Competition is a necessary ingredient of both failure and success.

Competition is fun – it's winning that's hard work.

For every failure there is a success – it just may not be one of yours.

The purpose of competition is not to win; it's to teach you how to lose.

"You can't win all the time" was spoken by a loser.

Man is a gregarious animal only because he can't be competitive all by himself.

Contentment is a fitting pastime – for a cow.

Folks seem to stick together only when somebody else is trying to tear them apart.

Competition is the only thing in the world that can make a winner.

The trouble with Communism is it doesn't have any competition.

Competition is the only justification for getting better.

COMPROMISE

Compromise," Daddy used to say, "is a subject on which a man has got to be willing to compromise."

That didn't make much sense to me when I was young, but as I got older I began to realize that, while there were some issues on which my Daddy stood firm and stout as a post oak, there were others on which he bent like a willow in the wind. At one point in my education, I remember, I had the audacity to question him about this seeming inconsistency.

He thought for a minute, and then he said, "Well, son, it's kind of like trading. If you got a brand new Barlow knife, it's the most important thing in the world to you. You just enjoy taking it out of your pocket and looking at it, and you wouldn't trade it for a pony. On the other hand, if a friend of yours should express an interest in an old fossil rock that's been lying on the bookshelf in your room for years, your first thought's gonna be: 'What has he got that I can trade it to him for?' Well, compromise is kinda like trading old fossil rocks."

"OK," I said, "I understand about trading old fossil rocks, but what about the Barlow knife? If somebody offered me a million dollars, I might trade it. And anyhow, it's gonna get old, and then I might want to trade it for a fossil rock."

"Yes," he said. "Some men would trade almost anything for a million dollars. And there are a lot of men who tend to forget what a thing is worth after they've had it awhile. But every man's got things that are not negotiable. There's always a point beyond which a man just can't back down – a kind of a line that marks the end of compromise. 'Course that line can vary from man to man, but the fact that it's there defines a man – and where it is defines the quality of a man."

We both thought about what he'd said for a moment or two while we watched a jet trail move several inches across a clear blue sky. Then he grunted and half shook his head. "There is one thing, of course, that a gentleman must never compromise. And that," he said as he looked at me and winked, "is a woman's honor."

Survival is spelled c-o-m-p-r-o-m-i-s-e.

Don't compromise what you can't replace.

The only folks that don't have to compromise are those that don't compete.

When most folks say "give and take," what they mean is: you give and I'll take.

Every time a man tries to straddle an issue, it jumps up and bites him on the butt.

There are two kinds of men that won't compromise: dead men and those that are about to become so.

Compromise marks the end of integrity – and the beginning of intelligence.

It may be true that oak trees don't compromise, but then oak trees never get anyplace but where they already are.

Don't compromise too much; victory and defeat are *both* good for you.

Every man has got to sell whatever he has got to sell.

Compromise is a two edged sword; it's got to cut slack both ways.

The mechanics of government is compromise.

Be careful you don't let compromise become a fancy word for giving up.

No man can serve more than one master, but a good man can service several mistresses.

Compromise is the cost of cooperation.

The right amount of compromise leads to consensus – too much leads to concession.

The end of compromise is commonality.

A man's got to compromise; it's just a question of whether he's gonna compromise something of his or something of somebody else's.

Compromise is the soul of negotiation.

A man that's willing to negotiate is willing to give up. Negotiation is just to find out how much.

There are no absolute negatives in negotiation.

Compromise in everything else, but never in the choice of a wife.

Where there is controversy there is merit on both sides.

Communication depends as much on listening as it does on talking.

CONCEIT

Art Yoder was probably the most conceited man I've ever met. His conversations were heavily spiced with the personal pronouns "I" and "me," and his whole demeanor seemed designed to call attention to himself. He wore diamonds on his fingers and an overcoat with a fur collar – unusual adornments for a man in the place and time I grew up – and he drove a midnight black Cadillac in which a boy could always see a grotesquely distorted reflection of himself. It seemed that Mr. Yoder, in breaking loose from the compulsory humility of his Amish upbringing, had swung like a pendulum to the opposite pole.

Daddy had undertaken the manufacture of a chicken medicator that Art Yoder had invented, and since Daddy's "factory" was in our garage, we had occasion to see rather a lot of Mr. Yoder around our house. Mama, who was always properly polite to Mr. Yoder when he was present, nevertheless made no secret of the fact when he was absent that she didn't like his "holier than thou" attitude. She was in the process of apprising my father of this aversion for probably the sixteenth or seventeenth time one Sunday afternoon over dinner, when Daddy, apparently "tired of hearin' about it," interrupted her by asking, "Honey, would you like another cup of coffee?"

Mama allowed that she would, and as Daddy was pouring it for her, he said, "You know Honey, nobody in their right mind deals with a man that's not conceited."

"You're right about that, Ed," Mama chuckled, and the subject was never brought up again.

I have always admired my Mama's perception, so eminently displayed on that occasion. As for myself, it wasn't until years later that I finally figured out what my Daddy had said.

Conceit is the easiest way to achieve ignorance.

Conceit is like good looks: a man can't get along without some, but too much is a sure sign of failure.

The greatest conceit in the world is modesty.

Only great men have humility – the rest of us have inferiority complexes.

Self-importance is the basis of survival.

Conceit is the only motive a man has for succeeding and the only excuse he has for failing.

A man's confidence rests on his abilities – his conceits rest on the abilities of others.

A conceited man has always got at least one admirer.

A man that thinks of himself too much relieves the rest of us from that obligation.

The more self-satisfied a man is, the less cause he seems to have.

It's amazing the number of people that wouldn't believe a priest on his deathbed but will swallow every word you tell them about how smart and good looking they are.

Conceit is the first form of self-deception that man invented, and it is responsible for all of the others.

The beginning of human understanding is the realization that you are not unique.

The major difference between conceit and deceit is that deceit is fooling somebody else.

Only inferior people see conceit in others.

Nobody likes somebody that's conceited – even if it's him.

Conceit has prevented more friendships than it's destroyed.

Folks always have more bad luck than good luck, because when they do have good luck, they call it skill.

It seems like the more important a man is, the more impotent he is.

'Man that claims he doesn't need the respect of others is suffering from too much self-respect.

'Fellow that talks too much about himself generally thinks too little about others.

If somebody's got to brag on you, who's better qualified than you?

Conceit is the only known antidote for stupidity.

He who loves himself too much respects himself too little.

Conceit is the basis of intolerance.

Public servants ought to be required to make all their decisions in the bathroom. It's hard for a man to be conceited with his pants down.

You can threaten almost anything a man has got – except his self-image.

There's nothing sadder than a man trying to live up to his reputation.

There's only one thing people care about other than themselves – their problems.

COURAGE

"Courage," Daddy used to say, "is not near as easy to spot as cowardice."

That observation reflects not only my Daddy's views on the difficulty of concealing cowardice, but his belief that courage is a very personal and private thing, not to be flaunted. Courage, to Daddy's way of thinking, was something you just had if you were a man, like testicles. It was a thing that a man required but not something that he talked about.

My Daddy had a lot of that kind of courage – the kind that usually doesn't show – the kind of courage that can make a man stand up and defend a helpless drunk against a bunch of bullies in a bar, or give money to somebody that needs it without telling anyone, or be willing to take the blame when it belongs to you.

But even though my Daddy never talked much about his own courage, he did have a few things to say about courage in the abstract. Most of these observations were cast in the mold of a demeaning humor, but there was almost always a grain or two of raw truth in them that, I like to believe, he intended for my education. Whether he did or not, however, that has been the effect.

Courage is whatever the hell it takes.

Fear is nothing more than the absence of confidence.

Bravery's mainly a matter of not having a whole lot of choices.

Courage is like clap: if you got it, you don't talk about it.

The only cure for fear is knowledge – preferably the knowledge of where the exit is.

Bravery is mostly a fear that somebody's going to laugh at you for being a coward.

Courage is doing what you got to do; bravery is doing what you got to do when you're scared.

Only cowards want freedom *from* things.

The only fear is the fear of being alone.

There are only two things in this world I'm scared of: tornadoes and politicians.

Bravery is due largely to a lack of imagination.

Being good is easy as long as you're not risking anything to do it.

There's no virtue without courage.

Fear is the father of hatred, and hatred is the father of cowardice.

We can be brave about facing the dangers we know; it's the ones we don't know that scare the hell out of us.

Danger is always where you least expect it; if it wasn't, it wouldn't be danger.

It takes a lot of courage to be patient enough to win.

There's only one thing that can keep a man from fulfilling his destiny: fear and doubt.

Dead heroes aren't brave – they're just dead.

I'd rather be remembered as a card carrying coward than as a dead hero.

You can do anything you want to do if you have faith – just make sure it's faith in yourself.

Fear may have started civilization, but it was courage that built it.

Being scared's nothing to be ashamed of – running is.

Only Captain Marvel and damn fools are afraid of nothing.

Courage is like a pocket watch: a man takes it out only when he needs it, not just to show it off.

The courage of the boy becomes the caution of the man.

Most of the confusion in the world is caused by not having the courage to ask questions.

Confidence comes from knowing what you're doing – bravado comes from knowing you don't.

Recklessness is not the same thing as courage, and caution is not the same thing as cowardice.

CRITICISM

To Daddy, criticism was a big part of being a father. He felt obliged, as I'm sure his father before him had felt obliged, to point out to his offspring each and every error in conduct or failure in demeanor that came to his attention. When I was quite young, I imagined – as I'm certain I was supposed to – that my Daddy was a kind of god, fully aware of all of my infractions and totally capable and willing to damn me to hell for the least of them.

It was only after I'd gotten older that I began to think of him more as a man and that, finally, on an occasion when I thought I was being unjustly criticized, I mustered up the courage to contradict him.

In the ensuing, tomb-like silence, I cursed my audacity and trembled before my fate. I remember wishing that I could somehow recall those brash words that seemed to hang, still ringing, in the air between us.

I suddenly realized that Daddy was smiling. My first thought was that he was smiling because he was going to enjoy hitting me. But he didn't hit me. He just turned his head to spit and then said, "You know, son, there is one thing a man has got to be able to do, and that's to take criticism. He doesn't have to *believe* it, mind you, but he *does* have to take it."

Criticism is generally intended to benefit the critic.

You can always tell what kind of man a fellow is by what he criticizes.

Some folks are doers – the rest are critics.

Most criticism is based on envy.

Insecure people don't take criticism well, and secure people don't take it at all.

The man that laughs at criticism is a man that knows what he's doing.

Anybody that's older than you are is a critic.

The easiest way I've found to handle criticism is to ignore it.

The critic is the last man that most folks listen to.

Most critics don't even know how to *do* what they're criticizing, let alone improve it.

Criticize the deed, not the man.

If it doesn't help get the job done, it's not constructive criticism.

Criticize is what people do when they can't teach.

If you can't advise, don't criticize.

Criticism should always be a means to an end – never an end in itself.

Most folks take criticism about as easily as they take castor oil.

Those who are wise don't criticize.

Never criticize a man for something you didn't do.

It won't help to criticize a man for something he couldn't help.

Critics and executioners have trouble finding friends.

Criticism's more likely to get you a fat lip than a fat purse.

Criticism can keep a boy a boy – or make one out of a man.

Never criticize a woman, never ever criticize a woman's sister, and never ever ever criticize a woman's kids.

Criticism is something a man reserves for his enemies and hides from his friends.

Everybody lives in a glass house – but some have more panes than others.

Don't throw stones if you don't like dodging rocks.

Critics are a dime a doesn't.

Doers do and critics criticize.

'Man that takes criticism seriously must know it's true.

Frustration is the father of criticism.

self-criticism is the key to creativity.

Criticism is a thankless job, but somebody's got to do it or nobody'll know what to think.

If you choose to live in a glass house, don't complain when people throw stones at you.

DEFINITIONS

My Daddy was not a lexicographer by any means, and it would be dishonest to pretend that what follows was written or spoken by him in the form in which it appears. His contributions to the enrichment of the language were almost always verbal and were usually on the order of: "You have a good day, now, hear? You know what a good day is, don't you? That's any day the end of the world didn't come – and you did."

Nonetheless, in preparing this book I felt that some of the things my Daddy said could best be presented in a dictionary format. Many of them were responses to situations that would be tiresome to relate, and not a few of them would be incomprehensible in their original form without detailed background information.

There follows, then, a lexicon of my own composition gleaned, however, from some of my Daddy's most vivid comments.

Accountability: A cheap substitute for responsibility.

Affluent: Owing more money to more people than most people.

Adversity: Something that happens to everybody but only benefits others.

Advice: Criticism disguised as philanthropy.

Ambition: A mental disorder that is normally transmitted to the male of the species from the female.

Anger: An emotional response to frustration, usually brought on by wives, children, or other superiors.

Antique: Anything that's older than I am.

Avarice: Greed that brings in an income in excess of five figures.

Cabbage: Texas Brussels sprouts.

Columnunist: A columnist who writes for the *New York Times* or the *Washington Post.*

Communist: A fellow that wants to share his dime and your dollar.

Conceit: Somebody else's pride.

Conscience: A euphemism for instinct.

Conservative: Somebody who prefers the problems we got to those that might be caused by their solutions.

Coward: A fellow who'd rather lose than take a chance of winning.

Creativity: A condition resulting from a lack of expertise.

Curiosity: The only thing that keeps most folks from just going out and ending it all.

Daylight Slaving Time: That time of year when it's still light enough outside to mow the grass when you get home from work.

Deceit: Something that everybody practices but nobody makes perfect.

Democracy: The belief that the dumbest man is as good at government as the wisest.

Dilemma: a mental block that keeps a man from seeing that he's always got a whole lot more than two choices.

Diplomacy: What somebody who says something to you and driving home six hours later you think, "Why, that man called me an SOB!" has got.

Discipline: The cost of freedom.

Discrimination: A thing that's admired in women but deplored by women.

Dixiecrat: A Southern Republican.

Ecology: A strategy to keep third world countries and poor people third world and poor.

Education: The systematic limitation of options.

Engineer: Somebody that, given enough time, can come up with an explanation for anything.

Expert: Anybody that reads regularly.

Equality: A fiction that politicians invoke in order to ensure their own inequality.

Facts: Things that we make up as we go along.

Fad: A trend that I am not involved in.

Fear: The absence of confidence.

Fetish: Somebody else's preference.

Firecrackers: Nachos with jalapeno dip.

Free: Something that somebody has already paid for.

Friend: Somebody that hates the same things you do.

Foreigners: Folks that talk funny and aren't running for office.

Frustration: Not being able to find anybody but yourself to blame.

Future: History that hasn't been written yet.

Good Man: One that dies before he's had a chance to do something for which he ought to.

Habit: The thing that makes a man's future just like his past.

Hero: A coward who's so afraid of being found out that he takes crazy chances.

Honesty: A subterfuge that people use when the expediency of lying is outweighed by the consequences of getting caught.

Ignorance: Any knowledge that doesn't match up with mine.

Impossible: Something difficult that I've got to do.

Income Taxes: The only thing that could make a Texan who works 70 hours a week pay to support some deadbeat in Massachusetts that won't work at all.

Intelligence: A euphemism for self-importance.

Jealousy: Hating somebody else for getting what you probably couldn't have handled anyhow.

Justice: A socially acceptable alternative to generosity.

Knowledge: A random collection of current opinion.

Lawyers: Folks that make fortunes off of other folk's misfortunes.

Legislation: The imposition of the prejudices of one group onto another.

Leisure: Something that most folks work so hard to get that when they do get it, they're too tired to enjoy it.

Luck: The natural result of hard work.

Manager: Somebody that knows how to get other people to do his work.

Managerie: A group of managers.

Marriage: Living together without all the sex.

Mediocrity: The stuff they print in the media.

Military Intelligence: A phenomenon that occurs with roughly the same frequency as legal ethics.

Mob: A society without an aristocracy.

Modern: Conforming to the latest fad.

Modesty: Giving other folks room to brag.

Native: Too lazy to move someplace else.

Neighbor: Somebody that the Bible says you are supposed to love and that you probably would if they didn't start their damn lawn mower at six o'clock on a Sunday morning.

Nobility: A degree of aloofness that is properly achieved only be thoroughbred horses and middle-aged Southern ladies.

Normal: What I am.

Opinion: An assertion of superior judgment.

Opportunist: Any one of your kids between the ages of five and twenty-five.

Opportunity: Something that I don't want to do.

Optimism: A chronic euphoria brought on by an acute lack of experience.

Optimist: A fellow that says," Some days are better than others;" a pessimist says, "Some days are worse than others."

Original: Something somebody else said or did so long ago that everybody's forgotten it.

Panhandler: Somebody from up north of Amarillo.

Patience: The ability to ignore what folks who think you are patient can't.

Patriotism: Having the right bumper sticker.

Perfection: An ideal condition attainable only by my children.

People person: a euphemism for technical cretin.

Person: A euphemism for woman.

Philanthropy: About the only thing you can do with money nowadays to keep from paying taxes on it.

Philosophy: The habit of casting the world in one's own image.

Phobia: Something somebody else is afraid of.

Politics: A kind of show business for comedians that don't have too much talent.

Political Science: What got Linus Pauling in trouble.

Prejudice: Anything you do to anybody who can accuse you of doing it because of prejudice.

Preposition: Something that illiterate people end sentences with.

Pride: The irrepressible conviction that you are better than anybody else.

Problem: An opportunity that you didn't take.

Procrastinate: To put off what you can't put off on somebody else.

Prudence: Giving a damn.

R&D: Ruin and damnation.

Rational: Having the same prejudices I do.

Regret: Giving a damn too late.

Reliable: Capable of lying to you more than once.

Ritual: A routine that nobody remembers the reason for.

Science: An accepted methodology for supporting one's opinions with experimental evidence.

Southern Metric System:

4 mites = a bit	10 messes = a bunch
8 bits = a passel	12 bunches = a bate
6 passels = a lot	13 bunches = a big bate
5 lots = a mess	

Tactrobat: Anybody that can stand on their own two feet without stepping on somebody else's toes.

Tacky: Having more than three of anything.

Televangelists' Followers: Born yesterday Christians.

Tolerance: Ignoring what you don't give a damn about anyhow.

Tradition: Something we keep doing because we've been doing it so long nobody can remember why.

Vanity: An attitude brought on by the constant fear that somebody might find out that you aren't even as *good* as your neighbor.

Victim: A Liberal euphemism for masochist.

Wall Street: A place where you can lose your money without having to fly to Nevada.

Wise: What many are called but few are proven.

Yankee: A Northerner that comes South.

Damn Yankee: A Northerner that comes South and stays.

Youth: That frustrating time of life when you've got all of the answers and none of the questions to match them up with.

DISCIPLINE

I think my Daddy's formula for "raising up kids right" would also make a good formula for building a healthy society. "A switch in time," he used to say, "saves crime."

While Daddy was certainly not averse to applying that formula when he felt it was needed, it was far from being the core of his method of discipline. "My job," he used to tell my brother and me, "is not to discipline you, but to teach you to discipline yourselves." To my Daddy's way of thinking, discipline wasn't something you imposed on a man; it was something that a man imposed on himself. It was one of the things that made him a man, but more than that, it was the thing that made him proud to be a man.

Daddy was a man of iron when it came to that kind of discipline. He was always a fair man to others, but a hard man on himself. You couldn't have paid him enough to make him cheat or steal from another man, yet when other men did those things to him, his response was disappointment rather than outrage. He was the product and the personification of the German discipline of his childhood, and I thank whatever gods there may be that he passed that legacy along to my brother and me.

A few of the things he had to say about discipline I have written down here, as much to renew my own appreciation of what he tried to teach me as to enlighten any potential seekers after truth.

Discipline is the price a man pays for freedom.

There are just three things that'll keep a man out of trouble: lack of ability, lack of opportunity, and discipline.

Discipline is something a man does to himself; what other folks do to him is punishment.

Discipline is a noun; it has never been a verb.

Discipline is the only means God gave us for making life endurable.

If you were to analyze the people you admire, you'd find that the thing *about* them you admire is discipline.

Discipline is what makes a man do the right thing even when there's nobody else around.

The fear of punishment is a poor substitute for discipline.

Luck is a nice thing to have, but skill is a whole lot more reliable.

The only difference between a smart man and a dumb one is discipline.

A man's ability depends on how much he's demanded of himself.

Discipline is like insurance: it may cost you to have it, but it's better than hoping you'll never need it.

God may forgive your sins, but nobody is going to forgive your carelessness.

Don't tell me what you think; show me what you can do.

Excuses are a sure sign of a lack of discipline.

Intuition is knowing what to do, tact is knowing when to do it, and discipline is knowing when not to.

Discipline may not be the greatest parent, but it sure does make a good chaperon.

A disciplined man has usually got more enemies than an undisciplined woman.

'Ever notice how luck just seems to hang around hard workers?

Self-discipline is the only kind there is.

I'd rather be late and right than on time and wrong.

The determination to do something is ninety percent of the job of getting it done; the other ten percent is just doing it.

Habits are like diapers: the dirtier they are, the harder they are to change.

Smoking is like breathing – it's easier to give it up altogether than it is to try to do it in moderation.

Discretion is doing what you want to do; doing what you have to do is discipline.

Always write with a pen; it teaches discipline. There are no erasers in the real world.

Sunrises may not be as pretty as sunsets but they're a whole lot better for you.

Discipline is what makes liberty out of license.

Time isn't something that flows by like a river; it's something that a man makes for whatever it is he has to do.

Discipline is minding your own business.

Discipline is doing what you really don't want to do.

Rules are made for people who don't want to think – and by people who don't trust them to.

Discipline may not keep a man honest, but it'll keep him too busy to steal.

Engineers and accountants both work with numbers. The difference is that engineers can't change theirs at the end of every month.

Discipline is the seed of trust.

The only good line is a deadline.

Changing your mind is not retroactive.

Luck is a four-letter word: w-o-r-k.

ECONOMICS

Daddy had no formal training in Economics, but that didn't keep him from having strong opinions on the subject. His appreciation of the "black art" – as he liked to call it – was not dissimilar to that of the art critic who only "knows what he likes," except that, in the case of Daddy's appreciation of Economics, what it usually came down to was that he knew what he *didn't* like.

In spite of his seeming lack of expertise, however, his observations in the Dismal Science were often startling and always thought provoking, and although he consistently mispronounced the names of both Keynes and Kondratieff, he knew enough from what he had read about them to know what they both stood for.

Some of what follows may seem dated to the modern reader, but if it does, be patient. If Daddy was right, it will all make sense again soon enough.

Economics is mostly the study of usury.

Economics is a method for the accumulation of selective statistics.

An Economist can prove anything you want to believe.

Economists are the modern equivalent of witch doctors. They shake out some old bones they call statistics, mumble some mumbo jumbo they call Keynsianism, and tell your fortune, which they call a forecast.

In the final analysis, all reasons are economic reasons.

Economics is the creature of greed.

The beginning of economic wisdom is the realization that gold and silver aren't commodities – currencies are.

The economy gets blamed for more human suffering than the devil ever did.

Economies are never out of control – they were invented by people and they are controlled by what people do.

Economics is always an effect – never a cause.

Economists only report what's happening – they don't make it happen.

All political decisions are based on economic decisions.

Government is the pimp of Economics.

Good Economics makes bad Government.

If Keynes was right about wanting the Government to control the economy, why was Marx wrong?

The Government prints money mainly so we'll have something to pay taxes with.

If it weren't for Economics, the Government wouldn't have any excuses at all.

Just because a thing is economically feasible doesn't mean it's economical.

Just because you can doesn't mean you have to.

Economic feasibility may not always be the first test of a proposal, but it should never be the last.

G. E. Kruckeberg

Economy is the last thing people think about and the first thing they complain about.

Keynsian economics has never been economical.

A cost-benefit analysis is a mechanism for emphasizing the benefits and minimizing the costs.

Capital is machines – not money.

Profit is the cost of capital.

An economy has a life, just like a man. It's born in investment, matures in saturation, ages in inflation, and dies in depression.

Depressions and booms are both caused by the same thing: interest.

Interest drives the economy.

The Industrial Revolution was made possible by usury – and so was the panic of 1837.

Interest creates new money, but the only thing that can create new wealth is more machines.

The health of an economy is measured by the rate at which people are buying new machines.

Inflation is what happens when the artificial money made by interest gets to be more than the real money made by manufacturing.

Economics is as dull as a rabbit pellet, and about half as useful.

If you think Economists know all about money, try asking one of them what it is sometime.

Either only crazy people become Economists or studying Economics just makes them that way.

EDUCATION

My Daddy's name was Edward, but everyone always called him Ed. I remember once a man in the barbershop asked him what Ed stood for. Daddy grinned that crooked grin of his, raked his fingernails across the stubble on his chin, and said, "Well, it sure don't stand for educated."

But my Daddy *was* educated. Even though his formal education went no further than high school, he never stopped learning. He was a voracious reader of everything from *Popular Mechanics* to the textbooks I brought home from school, and among the fondest memories of my childhood are those of sitting around the table after supper discussing with my father everything from aircraft propulsion to Greek Mythology.

Daddy had a great reverence for education, perhaps the more because humble origins, an early marriage, and the great depression had combined to rob him of the opportunity to pursue that elusive mistress to his satisfaction. But he was determined that my brother and I should not share that fate, and to that end he provided not only all the financial support he could afford, but through his perceptive advice and his persistent attacks on our sloth, abundant moral support.

A few examples of that advice are repeated below.

The purpose of education is to teach discipline.

Education is mainly a matter of learning good habits.

The birth of knowledge is the death of fear.

You can get knowledge from reading, but you get education from doing.

You can't learn algebra if you haven't learned to count.

You can't sail against the wind without a keel.

Education will teach you to read, but only discretion will teach you *what* to read.

You get wisdom from studying your mistakes; education is what you get from studying other people's mistakes.

Knowledge is valuable only as a guide to action.

The smartest man I ever knew was always going around asking dumb questions.

There is no fully educated man alive. A man keeps getting educated until he's dead.

Education is what you get from reading the instruction manual; experience is what you get from not reading it.

All a man's really got to know is how to learn.

An educated man is one that knows what books to look in to find the answers.

A man's got to know what's right before he can figure out what's wrong.

There's only one thing that can rob a man of his education: not using it.

A man learns mainly so he can teach.

Knowledge comes from listening; ability comes from doing.

Learn to listen to people. They may not ever say they told you so, but if they did, they told you only once.

You can't sell experience. In fact, you can't even give it away.

Experience is something that everybody has got to make for themselves.

Experience is like mash: it's not much good to anybody until after it's been distilled.

Every experience ought to be a learning experience.

Experience is something everybody's got plenty of, but nobody ever seems to have enough of.

A man that gets older without getting any smarter just hasn't been paying attention.

Experience is what we wish we'd had before we got it.

An education is mainly just a means of getting a job where you can learn something.

Degrees only open doors; once you walk through one, you're pretty much on your own.

A good education asks more questions than it answers.

A college degree doesn't give you all the answers – it just teaches you where to look for some of them.

A degree is the beginning of your education – not the end.

Education mostly just familiarizes a man with a lot of other folks' opinions.

Education is studying the past; intelligence is using what you learned from the past to predict the future.

History is a great teacher – and it's a dang good thing, 'cause it's the only one we got.

All knowledge is history.

We don't know anything that hasn't already happened.

Folks that haven't studied history are suffering from self-induced amnesia.

More than ninety-nine percent of what you know about yourself happened before you were born.

The value of history is that the lessons of the past can be applied in the present to control the future.

Education is the only way that civilization has of perpetuating itself.

Education increases conformity; it was never intended to increase intelligence.

Knowledge is not power – *using* knowledge is power.

Good teachers learn more than they teach.

Business schools don't teach you how to get your own business; they teach you how to give other folks the business.

Education is the great equalizer.

The progress of American educational philosophy in the last hundred years has been from disciplinarianism through child psychology to permissiveness – or from hickory to trickery to Spock.

Americans are the most over-educated people in the world – and the most poorly educated.

Universal education just means you've got to lower the standards so everybody can pass.

Those that can't teach have got to practice.

A teacher has got to have the patience of Job, the wisdom of Solomon, and the appearance of sanity.

Tenure means that you have got to kill a student before they can fire you.

Education is mostly a matter of learning to follow rules.

Innovation comes mostly from folks that aren't real familiar with the rules.

Education is spelled e-x-p-e-r-i-e-n-c-e.

Experience is what teaches a man to recognize a mistake when he makes it again.

FREEDOM

My Daddy's philosophy on freedom was simple: a man gets as much as he deserves. That was the dictum by which he raised my brother and me, and it represents a summation of his views on a wide range of subjects, from penal servitude to the amount of money he gave Mama at the end of each week. Freedom, in Daddy's world, was something you had to earn, and the way you earned it, curiously enough, was by giving up pieces of it.

Daddy understood intuitively that true freedom can only be attained through self-denial. He also understood that the appreciation of freedom, as well as its preservation, is not a passive but an active endeavor. Somewhere, I still have a letter that Daddy wrote to me when I was stationed in Korea, and I can still remember underlining the phrase that I think said all my Daddy ever wanted to say on the subject of freedom. "Freedom," he wrote, "is something that a man has got to keep working at."

Freedom is the price of security.

Free as a bird means free to be hit by cars, hunted by cats, and shot at by boys with beebee guns.

Freedom isn't something that somebody gives you; it's something that everybody is trying to take away from you.

Our freedom is most threatened by out desires.

A man deserves as much freedom as he knows how to use.

Every man is a slave to his own beliefs.

Freedom is the creature of growth.

Freedom is like a black eye: Nobody just gives it to you – you have got to fight for it.

Freedom comes not from a lack of commitment but from knowing that you will honor your commitments.

Liberty and liberalism are two sides of different coins.

Liberals are about as liberal as freedom is free.

Only slavery can give a man freedom *from* things.

Freedom just means that everybody has got the right to pick his own master.

The difference between freedom and license is that you've got to pay for freedom in advance – but it's a whole lot cheaper.

Crime is freedom without discipline.

No man can be free as long as another man is his slave -only women can.

Slavery never really got going on a big scale until the industrial revolution came along.

Opinion is the backbone of freedom because it's the one thing in all creation that everybody is entitled to.

Freedom is the price of progress.

Freedom precludes revolution. If you have freedom, you've got nothing to revolt against.

America has never fought a war that wasn't fought for freedom – but it was always for *our* freedom.

It's a free country – except for Manhattan; we paid $24 for it.

A man is free only to the extent that he doesn't threaten somebody else's freedom.

If you find yourself thinking about being free, you're probably not.

If the truth shall make you free, we're all in bondage.

Religious freedom in the United States means that you are free to embrace any brand of Christianity you want – assuming, of course, that it's Protestant Christianity.

You can't have religious freedom without having a little religion.

When most folks talk about religious freedom, they mean you can have *any* religion – they don't mean you can have *no* religion.

A man's free to do anything he wants, as long as he does what he's expected to do.

Slavery is possible only because a lot of folks think freedom is just not worth all the trouble.

FRIENDSHIP

I never realized how many friends my Daddy had until he died. It seemed to me at the time that there were thousands of people (though it must have been only hundreds) who came to pay their last respects to Daddy – and there were scores of others who sent regrets from as far away as Arizona and Michigan.

Many of the people who attended his funeral I hadn't seen in years, and there were more than a few there whom I'd never met at all. I remember in particular one old gentleman who came up to me after the eulogy to introduce himself. His hands had been roughened by a lifetime of hard work, and his face was leathered from many seasons of exposure to the sun. The double-breasted, dark blue pinstripe suit he was wearing smelled faintly of having hung in the back of a closet for a very long time. As he shook my hand, he said, "Your father was a good man. I'm proud he was my friend."

"Thank you," I said. "Daddy seems to have had a lot of friends. He must have done a great many things for a great many people."

The old man shook his head and smiled. "Son," he said, "a friend isn't somebody that does things *for* you; a friend is somebody that helps you do things for yourself."

I never saw that old man again – I'm ashamed to say I don't even remember his name – and I'm sure I shall never know what it was my Daddy helped him do for himself. But I know I shall never forget his definition of friendship, and I think, from some of the things I remember my Daddy saying about friendship, that it's a pretty accurate reflection of *his* feelings on the subject.

I would rather have a friend cheat me than for me not to have trusted him.

Familiarity breeds content.

Only a friend can disappoint you.

Your best friends are those you don't see a lot of.

Chose your friends wisely. A man is mostly what the people he's with at the time expect him to be.

Friendship is what makes life worth living.

A man is only as good as his friends.

It takes just two to make a friendship – more than that and you've got a game of follow-the-leader.

All good things must come to a friend.

Friendship is giving – taking is charity.

Most folks would rather have a friend than be one.

Respect is the cornerstone of friendship – but its foundation is self-respect.

A friend is somebody who would stand behind you if you were wrong and stand in front of you if your fly was open.

The main difference between rich folks and poor folks is that poor folks can tell who their friends are.

A friend in need is hopefully somebody else's friend.

Most folks aren't near as distressed by the misfortunes of their friends as they are by those of some stranger they read about in the newspaper.

The troubles of a friend can be comforting, because they tend to assure us that the chances of our having the same troubles are remote.

Never take advice from a friend: if it's good advice, you'll lose a friend; if it's bad advice, he will.

Your best friend in the world is the guy wearing your boots.

A friend is a foe with an ulterior motive.

The bonds of friendship are stronger than the bonds of matrimony – so you'd better make friends with your wife.

A man's friends become his family when his family quits being his friends.

Friends and foes may come and go, but family comes and stays.

If there is a hell, that's where I want to go – 'cause that's where all my friends are going to be.

When you try to buy friendship, you get only resentment for your money.

If you got a friend that you can't stand, just loan him money – and you'll never see him again.

Loyalty is only me deep.

Never tell a friend something that you don't want your enemies to know.

True friendships are rare, because there aren't that many true people.

Most friendships are sunk by their own torpedoes.

'The best way to keep a friend is to never tell him that you told him so.

Excessive friendship is the quickest way to make enemies.

Never tell a man what you think of him until you've both had at least two beers.

We usually like the folks that admire us better than the folks that we admire.

The best friendships are forged in war.

A friend is somebody you've been through things with.

A friend is somebody you never have to apologize to.

Enemies are better for you than friends, because they're a lot more stimulating.

Nobody's ever been betrayed by an enemy.

The quickest way to make an enemy is to laugh at a friend, and the quickest way to make a friend out of an enemy is to laugh at yourself.

You've got to be a friend to have one.

The best friends, like the best Christians, are converts.

'Man that depends too much on his friends makes his own enemies.

A friend in need is an enemy in seed.

Friendship is the only thing in the world that becomes more valuable the more you share it.

GOVERNMENT

Daddy came from a culture that placed a high value on discipline and authoritarianism. To the German mind, the state was an extension of the family, and the head of the state was imbued with all of the infallibility and assumptions of best interests that are normally ascribed to the father figure. Centuries of invasions and attempted invasions of the fatherland had taught the German people that a strong central government was necessary to their very survival, and that conviction had forged a nation capable of inventing Bismarck and William II and Hitler.

Yet that same culture gave birth to Luther and Kant and Einstein. It's always seemed to me that one of the greatest paradoxes of the German psyche is its simultaneous capacity for regimentation and rebellion, and that dichotomy was apparent in my Daddy's often contradictory feelings toward the Government. The same man who threatened to set fire to a hippie's jeans while he was still in them because the young man had had the poor judgment to sew the flag of the United States across the seat was fully capable of campaigning, at considerable effort and personal expense, for Strom Thurmond in '48 and George Wallace in '72.

Washington, so far as Daddy was concerned, was a necessary evil, but the emphasis in his mind was always on the second attribute. "Government," he used to say, "is like whiskey. A little bit might be good for you, but if you let yourself get addicted to it, it can kill you." Most of the other things Daddy had to say about the Government were in the same vein – designed, it seemed, to keep one ever mindful of the grave and ever-present danger of falling victim to that pernicious addiction.

G. E. Kruckeberg

A government is a bunch of people that we pay to take our money away and spend it to buy us things that we don't want.

The enslavement of the weak by the strong is natural; the enslavement of the strong by the weak is government.

The thing that makes democracy work is that 80% of the people are wrong only 20% of the time. The problem is that the other 20%, who are wrong 80% of the time, are running the government.

It's not the business of the government to keep us from making mistakes; it's our business to keep the government from making mistakes.

Democracy is the belief that the dumbest man is as good at government as the smartest.

You can't have a circus without elephants – or a braying contest without donkeys.

The majority may always be right, but the right is always a minority.

No government can govern without the content of the governed.

As long as you pay legislators more than they can make doing honest work, all of their legislation is going to be designed to keep themselves in office.

Unto everyone that hath shall be given, and from him that hath not shall be taxed away even that which he hath.

Taxes are the cost of graft.

What goes up must be a tax.

Paying taxes only encourages profligacy.

The reason congress is so quick to raise taxes is they can raise their salaries to cover it.

Throwing money at a problem to make it disappear will work every time. 'Course the *problem* will still be there.

The government's job is to make us happy; we can generally make ourselves miserable without any help.

There are two opposing theories in Washington. One says that we should take from the middle class and give to the poor and the other says that we should take from the middle class and give to the rich.

Ninety percent of the Offices, Bureaus, and Departments in Washington are fighting each other to see who can spend the most paying people to not work, and I think we could save a lot of money by consolidating them all into one agency. We could call it the Federal Underemployment Commission for Keeping Underprivileged People. At least the acronym would be appropriate.

'Fellow wouldn't mind the government spending so dang much for paper if they didn't turn around and make it worthless by printing money on it.

Democratic oppression is no better than any other kind.

Governments are a lot like religions: they send missions to foreign countries, they don't pay taxes, and they keep telling us we've got to sacrifice.

The government is always trying to catch you where you don't bitch.

If the government finds one nearsighted citizen, they want everybody to start wearing glasses.

Government exists by invasion of privacy.

Global solutions to local problems lead to global problems.

All of the ecofreaks are in Washington, because that's where all of the wild life is.

In Washington, the rule of survival is: judge not lest you be bugged.

Our government is a cancer – it was born on the fourth of July.

A society without an aristocracy is a mob.

There're a helluva lot more socialists in Washington than there are democrats in Moscow.

Capitalism and Socialism are just two different responses to the same thing – the Industrial Revolution.

The federal government's not all bad. It gives us someplace we can send our local politicians where the damage they do is done mostly to other states.

States don't have rights – only people do.

States' Rights is the only thing that holds the Republic together. Only a State politician could swallow federal politics without regurgitating.

No people in history has ever revolted against benign conditions.

Prohibition was an idea whose time was dumb.

Politicians live in the past mostly because they can't point to the future with pride.

Power corrupts, and obsolete power corrupts Congress.

The trouble with representative government is that the representatives never turn out to be what they represented themselves to be.

Government gets more protective because we keep inventing more things we need to be protected from.

Most folks would go for big brother if it didn't mean all the big bother.

Congress is a euphemism for getting screwed.

A Republican is a fellow that can't stand the heat and can't get out of the kitchen because he owns it.

The problem with representative government is that it suffers from *di*lution of responsibility and *de*lusions of grandeur.

A man can't avoid death and taxes, and the government can't afford to let the second get to the point where the first is preferable.

Those who think that government is part of the problem are wrong; government is *all* of the problem.

Some men want world peace; others want the world in pieces; but all in the world most of us want is a good piece.

GRATITUDE

"Thanks, Earl," Daddy said, as he reached out to shake the grimy hand of the wizened and sallow-faced mechanic. "I appreciate it."

Earl Wagner, sporting a three day's growth of beard and once-white coveralls that hadn't been laundered in over a week, ejected a charge of tobacco juice onto the oil stained dirt floor and said, "'At's OK, Ed. Anytime."

I reckoned at the time that it probably *was* OK by Earl, since Daddy had just handed him thirty dollars in crumpled ones and fives – more than the little alcoholic usually made in his back yard garage in a week – for less than a day's work. I knew that Daddy was being generous – doubtless for the sake of Earl's wife and four children – and I was sure that Earl knew it too. Furthermore, I was aware of a great many other things my Daddy had done for the Wagners over the years, like giving them vegetables from his truck patch or – on at least one occasion – bailing Earl out of jail.

As he backed the old Chevy out of the driveway, Daddy said, "Boy, that Earl sure knows engines. This baby's purring like a kitten."

"Yeah," I said, "but, shoot, Daddy, after what you paid him, why'd you have to go and thank him to boot. After all you done for him, he oughta thank you for *letting* him fix your car."

Daddy thought for a moment before he said, "Well, maybe you got a point, boy, but the way I see it that's Earl's problem. Y'know, gratitude isn't something a man earns – it's something he owes."

Many of the other things I remember Daddy saying on the subject reflect that same attitude. A few of these are listed below.

Gratitude is remembering what others have done for you and forgetting what you have done for them.

Thanks is cheap, but not as cheap as pride.

Gratitude is what folks have for what they think you're going to do – not for what you did.

Always thank a man, even if it's for something you did for him.

Gratitude in the poor is about as rare as generosity in the rich.

You can always tell a gentleman by the way he says, "Thank you."

Gratitude is ten percent humility and ninety percent nobility.

Thanks may be poor pay, but it's a dang good investment.

The most lubricious phrase in the English language is "thank you."

Gratitude is unpopular among folks who don't like to owe anything to somebody else.

Most folks would rather be known as willing givers than as grateful receivers.

If you don't like to thank people, just stop doing it – and before you know it, you won't have any reason to.

Vanity has only itself to thank.

Don't thank God for what He didn't do.

"Thank you" doesn't pay the debt; it's just a first installment on it.

Everybody's grateful for gratitude.

A man can't enjoy what he's not thankful for.

The best attitude is gratitude.

Complaining comes of having too much.

A man's got to be thankful for the little things, like his salary, the respect he gets from his kids...

When I was a kid, the thing I was always most thankful for was not getting caught.

Gratitude should never obligate a man to do anything that's against his principles.

Gratitude covers up a lot of faults.

A man just does what he's got to do, and if anybody's thankful for it, that's a bonus – but it's not necessary.

Don't let gratitude become an obligation.

If I could put thanks in the bank, I'd be a rich man.

Prostitutes always get paid up front, because they know a man's more grateful for what he expects to get than he is for what he's already got.

GREED

Daddy liked to tell the story about the Indian guide he met when he was fishing up in Michigan back in the early thirties. It was a simpler and less developed time, when two lane macadam was considered an improved road, and the upper peninsula abounded with bass-and-walleye-rich, pinetree-bound lakes that were virtually inaccessible by automobile.

The way Daddy told the story, he and the guide had hiked, with clothes and provisions on their backs, for three and a half hours to reach a one room lean-to cabin on the shore of a lake that only the Indians had a name for. The guide had been, even for an Indian, remarkably taciturn during the trek, and his loquacity did not increase as he went about gathering wood, starting a fire, and cooking their dinner of sourdough biscuits and beans. Finally, after they had eaten and were seated on opposite ends of a birch log in front of the cabin enjoying the lingering northern sunset and listening to the lonely calls of the loons, Daddy broke the silence.

"You don't like me much, do you?" he said.

The Indian just grunted.

"'Care to tell me why?" Daddy persisted.

The Indian rapped his pipe several times on the log between his legs, producing a shower of tiny sparks in the fading light. "White man too greedy," he said as he ground the sparks out with his boot. "When Indian fish, he put net half-way 'cross stream – always have plenty fish. White man put net all way 'cross stream – plenty soon nobody have fish."

"Every fish I caught on that trip," Daddy would say, "I turned back, except for the ones we ate."

The story, I believe, illustrates Daddy's feelings about greed on both the personal and the interpersonal levels. As he recognized and controlled his greed, he was also respecting the prejudices of the man who had pointed it out to him – a man whose own greed had led him into an occupation that he could only detest.

At least that's the way I see it. Of course, they were way out there in the Michigan wilderness, fifteen miles from the nearest farm, and Daddy never did say whether that Indian was bigger than he was.

Greed is what makes a man want more than he needs and need more than he wants.

Greed is wanting more than your fair share.

Praying for rain on your crops isn't greedy, but praying for drought on your neighbor's crops is.

The real sin is vanity – greed is just the evidence of it.

The prime mover is greed, not God.

Greed is the cause of wealth.

Greed is a disease of old men. When it does infect young men, it turns them almost immediately into old men.

Only a dang fool saves his money just so he can have a lot of it when he's dead.

Nobody's ever found a cause for greed. It's just something that some folks seem to be cursed with.

I'd rather be a slave to another man than a slave to my own greed.

The greedy may inherit the earth, but they won't be satisfied with it.

Greed is the cost of false pride.

The difference between avarice and greed is about six figures.

Greed is stupidity compressed into one syllable.

Nobody likes greedy people – they remind us too much of ourselves.

Greed is like whoring: a man's ashamed of it unless he's been real successful at it.

If the meek do inherit the earth, it'll only be because the greedy devoured each other trying to get it.

Greed may have built the British Empire, but it destroyed the British Empire.

Don't think about what you want; think about what you *should* be wanting.

Wanting and not getting is better than getting and not wanting.

It's not so much folks' greed for getting that bothers me so as it is their greed for doing.

The most powerful incentive in the world is jealousy.

When the needy outnumber the greedy, you've got an aristocracy; when the greedy outnumber the needy, you've got socialism; when the greedy and the needy are the same people, you've got a democracy.

G. E. Kruckeberg

HAPPINESS

The sun had set, leaving us afloat in the soft, gray placenta of a lingering summer twilight that was redolent with the smell of wet wood and water lilies. We seemed to be hovering, motionless as the blue-green dragonflies dimly visible against the darkening shore, in a timeless space between rose-tinted blue-slate water and burgundy-tinted blue-slate sky. Long, lazy swells heaved gently beneath our boat, like the sensuous breathing of a sleeping woman, and the seemingly endless silence that stretches from the last call of the turtle dove to the first screech of the owl was broken only by the creaking of our oars and the occasional splash of a jumping fish or a frog startled by our approach.

My young soul was overflowing with the dual joys of doing precisely what I wanted to be doing and doing it with the man I loved above all men in the world. "Daddy," I said as I worked a plastic crawler slowly through a bed of lily pads, "How come we can't always be this happy?" I paused to let the crawler sink for a few seconds at the edge of the lily pads before retrieving it. "And how's come people are ever unhappy anyhow?"

With a flick of his wrist, Daddy sent a Hula Popper whispering out over the surface of the water to land noiselessly somewhere in the blackness under the overhanging boughs of a big pine tree. He let the plug lie still for a slow count of five, then he jerked gently on his line, making a soft plup-plup sound. "Well," he said at last, "People are born happy, so I reckon that's their natural state. Unhappy seems to be just something that we do to ourselves."

I couldn't have been more than eight or nine years old at the time, but those words of my Daddy's keep coming back to me whenever unhappiness seems immanent in my own life. Daddy figured that unhappiness was a thing a man chose, that it was his own responsibility and his own business, and that the only thing another man owed him was a respect for that choice.

That philosophy is under heavy attack today. It is perceived as a self-serving attempt to alleviate one's guilt for the unhappiness of others. But guilt was a thing my Daddy never did dwell on. That would have compromised his feelings about himself, and my Daddy believed firmly that a man has got to feel good about himself. Because that, in the final analysis, is what happiness is.

A man's not measured by how happy he makes himself but by how happy he makes other folks.

Happiness is a job you've got to keep working at.

A man can't be busy and unhappy at the same time.

"Quality of life" is a contradiction in terms. Quality is being – and life is doing.

If you don't want to itch, don't scratch.

Happiness is having a problem to solve.

Happiness is now.

This is the future you gave things up for all your life.

Memories and dreams are just excuses for not doing what it takes to be happy now.

Happiness is mostly a matter of matching your ambitions and your abilities.

Happiness is a communicable disease.

Happiness is not asking a helluva lot of questions.

You can't buy happiness, but then if you can afford to, you probably don't need to.

Money can't buy happiness – or very dang much of anything else these days.

Problems are like opinions – they may all be different, but everybody's got them.

Only liars and idiots are happy all the time.

Success is getting what you want; happiness is wanting what you get.

To be happy, you've got to like yourself, love your wife, and adore just being alive.

A man's going to be here for only about 30,000 days, and today is the first one of the last of them.

There are two things that look bigger than they really are: anticipated trouble and expected pleasure.

Youth is the ability to enjoy.

Happiness is like lace: it's the holes in it that makes it pretty.

A man can't be happy all the time – his wife won't let him.

Happiness is a hot shower and a cold beer.

One way to find happiness is to be happy with what you find.

The true source of happiness isn't having – it's not wanting.

Happiness is the right woman.

A man can't be happy alone.

Happiness is a lot like love: the more you give to others, the more you get back.

The secret of happiness is having something to shoot for – or at.

If you want to be really happy, stay out of politics.

Happiness may be a warm puppy, but the degree of happiness depends somewhat on which end of the puppy is warm.

Happiness is cruising McAndrew Street in Modesto on Saturday night in a yellow deuce coup.

Happiness is knowing you could if you **had to** but you don't have to.

Happiness is waking up Saturday morning knowing you put the garbage out Friday night.

Happiness is learning.

Happiness is not being sorry.

Enjoyment is 10% adventure and 90% nostalgia.

The more you know about something the less fun you seem to have doing it.

Life's a series of propositions – happiness is accepting the right ones.

Happiness is appreciating the uniqueness of every experience.

Happiness is accepting the inevitable and being resigned to the impossible.

HEALTH

My Daddy was in excellent health right up to the day he died, and it has always been my opinion that he owed that enviable condition to continual and vigorous exercise. It was not that he deliberately worked out every day; it was more that healthy exercise was a natural by-product of the lifestyle he had chosen for himself.

That Daddy was aware of the healthful effects of that lifestyle was evident from a comment he made when I was home for Thanksgiving in my Freshman year at Purdue. Daddy and my younger brother were outside "tossing a ball around" and wanted me to join them. I, however, was immersed in a football game on TV.

"C'mon outside," my brother insisted. "You need the exercise."

"Yeah," Daddy added. "Ball games are like stag movies: it's a lot healthier for a man to do it himself than it is to watch somebody else doing it."

Daddy's attitudes on the healthful effects of some other common activities are apparent from the sampling of his remarks on the subject recounted below.

Exercise'll add years to your life. In fact it'll make you feel like it already has.

It ain't stress unless I want it to be.

Health seems to be something you get from giving up pleasurable activities.

Health is something a man starts chasing when he gets too old to chase women.

A man's health is like his wallet: he never thinks about it until he looses it.

An onion a day keeps the doctor away – and dang near everybody else.

Good health is a habit.

Staying healthy is easy: just don't get sick.

The concept of moderation is foreign to man. In war and in peace, the leading cause of death has always been suicide.

Your worst enemy is the guy that buys your cigarettes.

Quitters live younger.

Two helpings are for two people – or for somebody that wants to *look* like two people.

Giving up drinking won't make you live any longer, but it sure will make it seem that way.

The only problem I got with drinking is having to pay all the dang taxes on the stuff.

Good health is good humor.

Anybody that goes to a psychiatrist probably needs one.

Stress is anticipation.

Stress is caused by the delusion that you've got a choice.

If you want to live to be a hundred and ten, don't mix your whiskey and don't mix your women.

Health is something that young men take for granted and old men take offense at.

Sex is better for you than watching television – and a whole lot cleaner.

What I don't understand is how the desire to stay healthy can make folks want to ride bicycles in traffic.

Being in shape's like being in love: the more you are, the harder you have got to work at staying there.

I've noticed that the less a mechanic knows about the machine he's working on, the more he tends to charge. I guess maybe that's why doctors are so expensive.

Medicine is mostly a matter of treating the symptoms and charging the patient for as long as it takes for him to heal himself.

Doctors don't get paid unless they find something wrong with you.

A patient is somebody who's patient enough to stand still and not yell "rape" while some doctor is screwing him.

Physicians steal thy health.

It's not getting sick that scares folks so much as it is the certain knowledge that if they do, they will fall into the hands of doctors.

Medical practitioners are mostly still practicing.

The two major causes of death in the United States are overeating and underworking.

Snack and the world snacks with you; diet and you diet alone.

Early medicine men spent most of their time beating with a stick on an animal skin. Nowadays, they spend most of their time beating with a stick on a golf ball.

HONESTY

"Honesty isn't the best policy," Daddy used to say. "It's the only policy."

Those nine words represent the basis of my father's whole life: honesty. Honesty was the rock upon which he built his manhood, and it was the foundation upon which he insisted that I build my own. "When you lie," he used to tell me, "the only person you're cheating is yourself."

I don't mean to imply that Daddy was by any means a saint, or that he was immune to the duplicity that some have suggested is the natural heritage of mankind. There were indeed times – a few of which I personally witnessed – when my Daddy tried to lie. The problem was he couldn't. He had been schooled and had schooled himself for so many years in the rigors of honesty that his feeble attempts at falsehood were at best pathetic and unconvincing.

I don't think he ever realized this. I've heard him apologize years later for some imagined deception, apparently unaware that his attempt at falsehood had been transparent from the start. But whether it was due to a deep seated conviction or simply to the fact that he was a poor liar, Daddy was one of the most honest men I've ever known. And he taught me the real value of honesty: that it forces a man to be honest with himself. In Daddy's words: "Nobody likes a dishonest man – especially if it's him."

Honesty and courtesy are two sides of the same coin.

A man's only as good as his word, and his word is only as good as he is.

Folks will admire your honesty so long as you don't tell them the truth.

Honesty is a subterfuge that folks use when the consequences of getting caught outweigh the expediency of lying.

If you've got to tell a lie, tell one that'll make somebody feel good.

"The truth shall make you free" refers to what you say, not to what you hear.

A man that'll lie for you will lie to you.

Don't let a sleeping lie dog you.

Honesty is the best pretense.

Honesty is the offspring of conceit.   A fellow has got to have a pretty low opinion of himself to lie, cheat, and steal.

A white lie is one that *you* told.

Honesty may not always be the best policy, but it sure is the safest.

For most folks, lying is more a convenience than it is a vice.

Being honest shouldn't be that hard to do. You don't have a whole lot of competition.

The trouble with a lie is that if you tell it often enough, you start believing it yourself.

Nice people don't lie – they prevaricate.

Honesty is a boast fallacy.

'Fellow that says he's never lied has just added one more onto his record.

You can't lie to a man that's not a fool.

I'd rather be lied to than lied about.

The last person in the world you want to lie to is yourself.

It's not a lie unless somebody believes it.

Only a masochist gives an honest answer every time.

Honesty is never an acceptable excuse for rudeness.

Only a fool lies when he doesn't have to, and only a *damn* fool tells the *truth* when he doesn't have to.

Never trust a man that always tells the truth. He's up to something or he wouldn't be so dang careful.

An honest man is one that lies less than most folks.

A man that always tells the truth is either a fool or he figures you for one.

The more honest a man is, the less fuss he makes about other folks lying to him.

The lazy man is offended by sloth, and the liar by dishonesty.

Engineers are the most honest people in the world; they'll tell you everything they know and more.

An ounce of pretension is worth a pound of truth.

Muddy water always looks deeper than clear water.

'Fellow that swears he's telling the truth is lying sure as the devil.

Competition is the only reason for honesty.

Nobody ever argues for the truth. He argues for what he wants to believe.

Nobody really likes old dogs or honest people.

Everybody is lying to you; it's just that some folks are better at it than others.

The only difference between a lie and the truth is the percentage of people that believes it.

It's amazing the number of people that wouldn't believe a priest on his deathbed who will swallow every word you tell them about how smart and good looking they are.

Flattery may not always get you no-where, but it dang sure can get you someplace you don't want to be.

You can win with honesty or lose with honesty, but you always lose with flattery.

Flattery is honesty embellished.

Blarney is Irish for BS.

The trouble with honest people is you can't trust 'em.

Honest people can still be very inventive; after all, they invented dull.

Honesty and politics don't mix.

An honest man is the noblest work of his press agent.

Lie is both a verb and a noun, but there is no verb for telling the truth. I guess maybe we never needed one.

The only difference between a crooked fellow and an honest fellow is the crooked one got caught.

Don't believe everything you hear from pathological liars and news reporters.

The more a man insists on something, the more sure you can be that it's not true.

The only thing anybody can guarantee you is that there are no guarantees.

A man that's not willing to lie is not willing to win.

Pessimists always call themselves realists, and realists always call themselves optimists.

Most folks spend more time justifying their mistakes than they do correcting them.

Everybody lies, but some of us are more straightforward about it.

The secret to domestic tranquillity is dishonesty.

HONOR

There was a war waiting for me in Asia and a girl waiting for me at home and a whole world waiting for me to get my degree and start showing them how engineering ought to be done. The word "fragmentation" was taking on a new meaning for me, and despite the level of maturity normally attributed to the average college sophomore, this sophomore felt about as mature as an unripe turnip – and not half so competent at making honorable choices.

As always, when confused and feeling unsure of myself, I sought out the advice of the wisest man I knew – my father. After listening patiently for several minutes, he said, "Boy, your trouble is you're worrying too much about what other folks are going to think. The only honorable thing to do is what *you* want to do."

I made the decision I really wanted to, and I am confident even today that it was an honorable one, at least according to Daddy's definition. "Honor," I can remember him saying, "has got nothing to do with other folks. A man can only be dishonorable to himself."

Honor is being what you seem to be, and not seeming to be what you're not.

Honor is courage in reserve.

They say there's no honor without justice, but if we had justice, we wouldn't need honor.

There is only one person in the world that you have really got to please: the fellow in your shaving mirror.

Honor is that degree of egotism that keeps a man from doing something embarrassing.

Honor's just a big word for being more concerned with the welfare of others that you are with your own.

Honor is what separates the other animals from man.

Honorable is how a man acts, not who he is.

You can't buy honor; and if you could, it wouldn't be honor.

I'd rather be remembered for my own honor than for that of my ancestors.

If you're going to give something to somebody, don't put your name on it.

Honor is not so much a debt we owe to those who came before us as it is a debt we owe to those who come after us.

Honor is what folks give you when they owe you and they don't want to pay you.

When somebody gives you the honor of doing something, it's usually something that they don't want to do.

Honor is what people have left when they don't have any money.

Honor is ten percent self-respect and ninety percent respect for others.

Too many times honor is just a handy excuse for doing something stupid.

More atrocities have been committed in the name of honor than of hatred.

You can always tell an honorable man because he never has a whole lot of friends.

A man that makes a big thing about being "honor bound" is usually a bounder.

The easiest decision is almost never the best decision.

There's no honor among chiefs.

HUMOR

My childhood sense of humor was honed on the Sunday funnies and Laurel and Hardy movies. I delighted in the slapstick, in the banana peel on the sidewalk, and in the resilience of Elmer Fudd who, though blasted by dynamite and smashed by two thousand pound anvils, always managed to return, seemingly unscathed, to his eternal pursuit of that "wascal wabbit." Although I didn't realize it at the time, humor to me was the enjoyment of someone else's suffering, and had it not been for Marlene Shields, I might have persisted in that delusion.

Marlene and I shared the same Sunday School class, though we had little else in common except that we were both at that age when, for some obscure biological reasons, the sexes are at constant war with each other. The occasion of a church picnic in honor of Independence Day would not ordinarily be expected to alleviate that conflict, and the fact that it did was attributable more to the insight of my father than to the effects of either piety or fried chicken on the maturity of the two combatants involved.

Our church was set well back off the road, with a huge grove of weeping willows behind it and a broad, sweeping lawn in front, where the Ladies Aid Society had set out long tables and folding chairs for the annual event. After we had all partaken more than our fills of Swiss steak and wieners and kraut and kartoffel salad and samples of each of the scores of deserts presented, and while the grownups were taking their ease and sipping iced tea, I decided to open another chapter in the long-standing war between Marlene and myself.

There was a rigid ritual to these encounters, by the rules of which a boy expressed his interest in a girl by calling her a fat, ugly pig, or some other epithet equally calculable to arouse the ire of a pubescent female, and then ran away laughing. The girl, by the rules of the game, was then obliged to chase the offending male, although both participants knew she was never supposed to actually catch him. I've forgotten what it was I said to Marlene that day, but it was obvious from the seriousness of her pursuit that I had struck a nerve, and that she intended not only to catch me but to beat the hell out of me.

As I rounded the corner of the church and headed flat out for the willows, I could hear Marlene's feet pummeling the ground close behind me, and I fancied I could feel her breath on the back of my neck. I leaped for the lowest branch of the first willow, swung myself up, and with hands and feet working feverishly managed to scramble up to about twelve feet above the ground, where I paused to look triumphantly down. I expected to see Marlene standing helplessly on the ground shaking her fist at me; what I saw was Marlene climbing up after me.

Then an amazing thing happened. As Marlene brought her full weight to bear on a limb some five feet below me, it came loose from the tree with a loud snap, and it and Marlene landed together on the ground below. My laughter, accentuated by a sense of relief, was uncontrolled. But it was short-lived. My own footing turned suddenly to air, and I was aware of a curious sensation of weightlessness. A moment later I was lying on the ground entangled in the branches of the limb on which I'd been standing, with Marlene's hysterical laughter ringing in my ears.

My father seemed to appear instantly, no doubt in response to my cries of distress. After assuring himself that neither of us had broken any bones and that the major damage had been to our dignities, he exercised the perennial curiosity of adults by asking us to relate our separate versions of the events leading up to this debacle.

After listening to "well-he-this" and "well-she-that" for half a minute or so, Daddy held up his hand and said, "Whoa, now, just hold on a minute. It sounds like both of you need to learn that it's not nice to laugh at other folks. Y'know, one of the nice things about being human is we can laugh at ourselves. Laughing at somebody else is something any hyena can do. Now you two just shake hands and make up."

As Daddy walked back around the corner of the church to re-join the adults, Marlene stuck her tongue out at me. For some reason, I just laughed.

If you can't laugh at yourself, other folks will do it for you.

Funny is like free – it's at someone else's expense.

The best humor is masochistic.

A sense of humor is what keeps a man from getting mad when the jokes on him.

Humor is the measure of a man.

Don't ever be the first one to laugh. It might not have been a joke.

It's not funny if you're the only one laughing.

A joke's like a carnival mirror: it's only funny when you can see yourself in it.

The best way to make a point is with a ridiculous example. Folks will remember a thing longer if it made them laugh.

Hope springs eternal in the humor of jest.

There's a name for people that don't have a sense of humor: paranoid.

Paranoia is a progressive disease: the more paranoid you act, the more people really are out to get you.

Levity is the soul of sanity.

Good health is good humor.

Keep looking for the silver lining, and you'll get cataracts from the ultraviolet radiation.

The quickest way to gain a friend is to laugh at yourself; the quickest way to lose one is to laugh at him.

A sense of humor is a sure sign of intelligence.

Humor is the appreciation of absurdity. I guess maybe that's why only humans have it.

G. E. Kruckeberg

A sense of humor doesn't mean a man doesn't take things seriously; it means he doesn't take *himself* seriously.

Humor is often a disguise for prejudice.

Laughter always makes you feel better – particularly if you're laughing at somebody else.

Laugh and the world laughs with you; cry and they'll laugh *at* you.

There are two things you never want to laugh at: an IRS auditor and a woman.

A sense of humor is the ability to laugh at yourself as hard as other folks are laughing at you.

Laughter may not be the best medicine, but if you laugh at the wrong person, it could turn out to be the most expensive.

A joke is the noblest work of man.

One odd pun deserves an odder.

The truth is always funnier than anything you could make up.

A sense of humor is mostly a sense of destiny.

If you don't want folks to laugh at you, don't act funny.

The best way to keep from regretting your mistakes is to laugh at them.

The reason that women cry and men don't is that men laugh instead.

Humor is funny. And the farther you are away from it, the funnier it is.

INTELLIGENCE

Daddy believed in intelligence. It was the one thing he admired in a man and his most important consideration in judging one. "Intelligence," he used to say, "is the only thing that differentiates a man from his horse."

Daddy also believed, as one might expect a man whose ancestors had cleared and conquered a savage land to believe, that a man is always capable of improving himself. These two beliefs led his always consistent mind to the inevitable – though even today unpopular – conclusion that a man's intelligence is not fixed, but is a continually evolving entity that is amenable to expansionary efforts.

I think that deduction was an unconscious one, and Daddy would no doubt have given lip service to the theory of innate intelligence had anyone asked him. Still, there is ample evidence to suggest that he believed otherwise – evidence to be found in some of the admonitions he encumbered me with as I was growing up. Although these were given in no perceptible order and with no observable philosophical underpinning, I believe they were the outcroppings of a bedrock belief in the basic perfectibility of humanity.

A few of what I consider to be – or at least what I have personally found to be – the more valuable of these admonitions, I have arranged below in a sequence of my own device. Adherence to these seven rules will almost certainly improve anyone's level of intelligence, and I would urge the reader to study them – even to memorize them – since a higher level of intelligence will, I believe, greatly enhance your appreciation of the rest of this book.

1. Read for at least an hour every day–
   intelligence has got to be fed.
2. Set goals for yourself – they're the
   whetstones of intelligence.
3. Push yourself – ability is only
   proportional to demand.
4. Predict the outcome of everything you
   plan to do – or not do.
5. Analyze everything you see, hear, and do–
   never stop asking why.
6. Don't make dilemmas out of problems – you've
   always got more than two options.
7. Avoid habits – they desensitize the mind.

A few of some of the other things – probably less coherent but perhaps more entertaining – that Daddy had to say on the subject of intelligence are given below.

Just 'cause a man is wrong doesn't mean he's not intelligent.

A man's intelligence is measured not by how much he knows but by how much he's willing to tell.

To most folks, intelligent means what they are.

Intelligence is the ability to see more than two choices.

It's easier to have an opinion than it is to verify one.

Folks have opinions about what they don't know.

Everybody is ignorant – they're just ignorant about different things.

Ignorance can be cured, but stupidity can only be endured.

Knowledge doesn't make a man intelligent any more than ignorance makes him stupid.

Intelligence is thinking about what's going to happen so it won't.

Intelligence is only as good as what it's got to work against.

The main reason for being intelligent is other folks are.

There's only one substitute for intelligence that I know of, and that's keeping your mouth shut.

Intelligence isn't remembering so much as it is knowing what to forget.

If you're not smart, you gotta be careful.

'Fellow that rests his argument on authority isn't thinking – he's just remembering.

Reasoning is asking why.

Thinking is so rare that when we see it we call it genius.

You'll find that people attribute good sense mostly to those that agree with them.

Intelligence is a lot like modesty: folks that tell you they've got it don't.

If a man is really smart, he knows his biggest advantage is that everybody else thinks they are smarter than he is.

Intelligence won't make a man happy, but it will make it easier for him to tell when he's not.

Some folks think intelligence is mostly instinct, but my observation has been that it's mostly extinct.

Just 'cause you know it doesn't make it true.

Intelligence isn't measured by how much a man knows, but by how long it took him to figure it out.

Intelligence is appreciated only by those who have got some of it.

Some folks say man is the most intelligent animal on the planet. Some other folks think that's not true, and maybe for them it's not.

Intelligent is how a man acts, not what he is.

There is a point in any organization beyond which the display of intelligence is unwise.

Organization is a poor substitute for intelligence.

Consistency is not a sign of intelligence.

Strong has never been a good substitute for smart.

Ignorance knows everything – except itself.

Intelligence is mostly a matter of considering the alternatives.

Ignorance is voluntary.

Assumptions should always be considered guilty until proven innocent.

Folks that shoot themselves in the foot usually aren't smart enough to be handling firearms in the first place.

Intelligence and humor both spring from imagination.

The human mind is a wondrous machine for discovering the obvious.

It's not what you know, it's what you think about it that counts.

Great minds run in the same ruts.

The function of logic is to justify what we already did.

The mind is a Teflon trap.

Ignorance is not knowing; stupidity is knowing and doing it anyhow.

The major cause of stupidity is laziness.

Experience is the only cure for ignorance.

Stupidity is doing the same thing again and expecting different results.

JUSTICE

When I was a boy, I was blessed – or cursed – with an insatiable hunger to read. It was not that I had any great desire to acquire knowledge, mind you. It was simply that I enjoyed reading. I would read anything, from the side panels of cereal boxes at the breakfast table to the yellow newspapers in which the Christmas ornaments had been wrapped the year before, and if Mama found any fault in me at all, it was only that I was always reading when I was supposed to be doing something else.

Fascinated as I was by the power and beauty of the written word, I suppose it was only inevitable that I should be victimized by it. But victimization is a strong word. My affliction was voluntary, brought on by an obsession for the verbal wizardry of the advertising copywriter. I was a pushover for advertisements – the kind of advertisements that appear on the back covers of comic books and in the back pages of *Boy's Life* magazine – advertisements that prey on a boy's overactive imagination and his thirst for recognition and glory. Lured by half-truths and vague promises, I would eagerly send off my hard-earned lawn mowing money for a book of magic or a pair of X-ray glasses, then haunt the mailbox every day for weeks, while my mind conjured up visions of dumbfounding people with brilliant slight-of-hand or of being able to see through girls' dresses.

I was often disappointed but seldom deterred. I knew there had to be a whole, big, enchanted world out there, with exciting addresses like New York Central Station and Hollywood, California, that could somehow make all my dreams come true via the magic highway of the U. S. Post Office Department.

Then, at the mature age of fourteen, I found the perfect vehicle for the realization of those dreams in a full page Sunday supplement ad for a book club. The only problem was that you had to be eighteen to join, or – in fine print at the bottom of the page – you could get your "parent or guardian" to sign for you. Confident in my Daddy's ability to recognize an almost obscene bargain, I took the ad to him and asked him to sign the coupon in the indicated space so I could clip it out and send it in.

To my amazement, he barely glanced at the ad before casually shaking his head and returning to his perusal of the comic section.

"But, Daddy," I protested, "I can get three free books."

"But you gotta buy a book a month for the next year," he said, "and I guaran-dang-tee you the cost of those twelve books will more than make up for the first three."

"But," I persisted, "it says right there that the first three books are free."

"Boy, let me tell you something," he said. "The only thing that's ever free is something that you have already paid for."

I remember suddenly realizing that Daddy was not talking about mail order book clubs. He was talking about justice, and how it applied to the making of decisions. "A man gets what he pays for," he used to say, "and he pays for what he gets." Daddy saw justice as a force of nature, as powerful and inevitable as gravity. It was a force that ultimately called a man to account, and Daddy believed that a man had a responsibility to himself to make intelligent choices – choices in how he spent his money and his time and his life.

There is another justice that Daddy sometimes talked about – or more accurately joked about. It's what is usually referred to as human justice. I have included here his comments on both.

In this world, you get just what you ask for – whether you want it or not.

Justice is like rain: you're going to get it sooner or later. The only question is when and how much.

Man didn't invent justice, he just made it obvious by inventing *in*justice.

Fate is justice.

Justice is whatever a man deserves.

Life may not always be fair, but it's always just.

Justice is an easy mistress but a hard master.

A really just man is really just a man.

God is just – man just is.

Justice is never an option. It's always a certainty.

Mercy and justice are natural enemies.

The sins of the fathers shall be visited on their fathers' sons.

It doesn't make any difference whether you give justice or injustice; what you get back is always justice.

Justice doesn't care so much what you do as what you did.

Justice can be neither bought nor bought off.

Everybody wants justice, but most folks want it just for themselves.

"Justice for all" means give it freely to us and impose it on them.

Justice is a euphemism for revenge.

Justice is the only virtue we really need; the rest of them are just there to help us bear injustice.

Justice is never given as freely as it's taken.

Human justice may not always be fair, but it's not near as unfair as human injustice.

Justice may not be blind, but she sure does seem to need glasses sometimes.

Justice may not always be just, but crime is always criminal.

A man that'd kill his own kind would be better off if he was dead – and the rest of us *sure* would be.

Whosoever taketh man's life, by man shall he be protected against cruel and unusual punishment.

The main premise of the American Justice System seems to be that the innocent are guilty, and that therefore the guilty must be innocent.

Some of our judges seem to think that it's all right to pay the fiddler with a dance.

The parole system was invented by judges so they'd be sure of always having a job.

Justice is whatever you can afford.

If it's something somebody gave you, it's a gift; if it's something you had to fight for, it's a right.

Justice is the legacy of the strong.

You can have justice without peace, but you can't have peace without justice.

Justice is as much as you can take.

Where I come from, it takes longer to convict a man than it does to hang him.

The grim reaper is an old man who sowed a lot of wild oats when he was a young man.

As you grow so shall you weep.

A man is never more just than what he has to be.

The payment for injustice is always justice.

G. E. Kruckeberg

LAWS

The word "laws" as used here has nothing to do with the regulations that are dictated by legislators and turned so readily to profit by the legal profession. Nor does it refer to the observations that are proffered by the scientific community as "natural" laws. What is presented here might more properly be called theories than laws. They are intended more as suggestions of the possible nature of the human experience than as hard and fast rules, and they are offered more for consideration and discussion than as dogma.

They were certainly never issued by my Daddy as either proclamations or revelations, but were simply given as comments on specific occasions. The format in which they are here presented is mine (although I owe much to that greatest of all legislators, Murphy) and it has been designed as much to enhance the reader's enjoyment as to assist the author in their codification.

Rules of Accountability:
1. Never do anything you can't blame on somebody else.
2. If they can't blame you for it, it's not your problem.

The Law of Antigravity: It's easier to pick up a woman than it is to drop her.

Archimedes' Principle: A man will displace a volume of progress equal to the weight of his influence.

cat attacks, retreat.
3. That was then; this is now.

The Categorical Imperative: It is imperative that everybody fall into some category.

The Law of Diminishing Returns: It's always yours that do.

The Three Rules of Domestic Tranquillity:
1. Don't ever disobey your wife.
2. If you do, don't let her find out.
3. If she finds out, plead drunkenness.

Murry Einstein's Theory of Relativity: The more money you make, the more relatives you have.

The Golden Rule: If you can get the gold, you get to make the rules.

Sam Gresham's Law: Bad news drives out good news.

The Inverse Square Law: If you act inversely, folks will think you're a square.

The First Law of Journalism: Good news is no news.

The Law of the Jungle: If you're not built like Johnny Weismuller, don't try to play Tarzan.

The Kent State Axiom: If you throw rocks at men with guns, you have got to expect to get shot at.

Kruckeberg's Laws:
1. Nothing ever changes – things just go from one extreme to the other.

129

2. Opposition and dissension are the cause of everything.
3. You always get out less than you put in.

Land's Law: The money's in the film, not the camera.

The Rules of Management:
1. Delegate.
2. If you can't delegate, procrastinate.
3. If you can't procrastinate, find somebody else to blame.

The Laws of Crisis Management:
1. To overcome a crisis, you must first create one.
2. Don't panic; it makes you look like you don't know what you're doing.
3. Delegate responsibility, never authority.

Abe Mendel's Law: If you got red hair and she's a blonde, your chances are 66 2/3% of losing a paternity suit.

Rocky Newton's Law of Gravity: The gravity of any situation is directly proportional to your involvement in it.

Rocky Newton's First Law of Motion: Never make a motion except for adjournment.

Rocky Newton's Second Law of Motion: No matter who made the motion, if you second it, everybody'll blame you.

Rocky Newton's Third Law of Motion: Only a third of your employees are ever in motion at the same time.

Max Ohm's Law: There's always resistance to anything current.

Jerry Parkinson's Law: The money supply will expand to fill the available debt.

Leo Pareto's Rule: 20% of the people cause 80% of the problems.

Ralph Pascal's Law: The pressure's the same no matter where you go.

The Perversity Principle: If you are trying to find something, it'll always be in the last place you look.

The Laws of Corporate Politics:
1. Never solve a problem if you can blame it on Somebody else.
2. Always have a job description so you'll know what's not your job.
3. Never communicate verbally if you can copy at least four people with a memo.
4. Never do anything you won't get credit for.

The Procrastinator's Motto: Tomorrow is the first day of the rest of your life.

The Principles of Operations Research:
1. The people who know what's wrong won't tell you.
2. The people who tell you what's wrong don't know.

The Laws of Organization:
1. Systems don't work.
2. People work.
3. The way they work is against each other.

The Law of Patronage: A program is only as weak as its strongest proponent.

The Law of Probability: If you've got a fifty-fifty chance of getting a thing right, you'll get it wrong every time.

Reagan's Rule: Always play to your audience.

The Law of Serendipity: When you're looking for a word in the dictionary, you'll learn at least two new words and forget what the word was you were looking for.

The Law of Supply and Demand: The more you supply, the more they demand.

LAWYERS

Daddy didn't care much for lawyers. "The dregs of propriety" he used to call them. I can still remember the day – I must have been about ten at the time – that Daddy took me with him to visit a lawyer's office. This was not a normal occurrence, and I'm sure the only reason for my being there was that Mama was otherwise occupied that day and had charged Daddy with the responsibility for my welfare.

The subject of the conversation between Daddy and the lawyer was probably beyond my comprehension and certainly beyond my interest. I remember that I was occupying myself in flipping through old issues of *National Geographic* magazine looking for pictures of women with naked breasts when the lawyer, for some reason, brought up the subject of ethics.

"Ethics?" I recall Daddy snorting. "Hell, Sam, it's just a dang good thing that doctors don't have the same ethics you lawyers do, or we'd all be subjected to germ warfare."

The lawyer did what lawyers do best – he made mollifying noises – and Daddy became mollified, leaving me to slip back into my own fantasies.

That event, trivial as it may seem, apparently made an indelible impression on me, and over the years I have often had those words pop back into my mind – usually when I am dealing with or am about to be dealing with a lawyer – and I believe they have been instrumental in preventing me from confusing ethics with the objectives and practices of attorneys.

Most of what Daddy had to say about lawyers was in the same demeaning vein, and I have set down here, as much to warn the unwary as to entertain the unwitting, a sampling of those pithy insights.

A lawyer's just a big expense looking for a problem.

An attorney is somebody that makes a fortune out of other folks' misfortunes.

Lawyers are a law unto themselves – and a flaw unto society.

Legal ethics is about as common as military intelligence.

There *is* honor among thieves: they call it legal ethics.

If justice weren't so dang blind, it wouldn't be so easy for lawyers to trip her up.

Justice isn't blind; lawyers are just nearsighted.

Underprivileged people are those who can't afford lawyers.

A good lawyer is one who believes in no arrest for the wicked.

The English call lawyers solicitors; over here, that's what we call hookers.

Lawyers are like prostitutes: They can sell what they got and still have it.

Lawyers and fools follow the rules.

The shills of the law mine the lowly, but they mine increasing crime.

Lawyers keep the law – and a third of the money.

The major occupation of the legal profession seems to be figuring out ways to guarantee that folks will have to keep on hiring them.

Whether their clients win or lose, the lawyers always win.

The reason lawyers charge so much is that they have to spend so dang much time waiting for judges.

The worst thing about getting sued is that you have got to go out and hire yourself a lawyer.

Successful lawyers tend to go into politics – I guess because they figure they can do more damage there.

There ought to be a law against lawyers becoming politicians. That's like a dogcatcher becoming a dog breeder.

A lawyer is accountability in action.

Lawyers like to use Latin a lot because it makes it harder for you to figure out what they're doing – and harder to figure out that they don't know either.

Precedent is a legal principle that says if you let somebody do it to you once, you have got to keep on letting them do it to you.

The legal and medical professions prey on each other: lawyers sue doctors for alleged malpractice, and doctors charge lawyers high prices for allegedly necessary surgery.

One of the tragedies of our time is that a man can get richer suing people than he can curing them.

LIFE

"Life's a lot like riding a bicycle," Daddy used to say. "It's easy as long as you're going someplace. But if you ever stand still, you'll fall flat on your prat."

That observation is a fairly accurate summation of Daddy's views on a subject that is easily the most debated in all of the history of human literature and philosophy: life. To my Daddy, life was just working and loving and playing and hating and thinking and eating and drinking and getting drunk and going to church and raising kids and spoiling grandkids. Simply being, to Daddy's way of thinking, was a luxury that only a rock could afford. Life is synonymous with survival, and survival for all living organisms is synonymous with activity. I happen to think, with all due respect to a host of seeker-after-the-truth from Saint Paul to Jean-Paul Sartre, that after two thousand years of writing and discussing and arguing about the meaning of life, my Daddy finally got it right – Life is doing.

I don't think Daddy ever read Aristotle's *Poetics*, but if he had, I'm sure his favorite quotation from that work would have been one that I have always found to be particularly inspiring. "Life consists of action," Aristotle said, "and its end is a mode of activity, not a quality."

But before someone reminds me that you didn't buy this book to read Aristotle, let me proceed to more of what my Daddy had to say on the subject.

The purpose of life is living.

The meaning of life is what you put in it.

God gave man life so he would have the time it takes to improve himself.

The only way a man can keep from stumbling is to give up walking.

Risk and ye shall be given.

Lovers may care and losers may share, but winners will always dare.

Life is the enjoyment of it.

Life is like climbing a tree: the higher you go, the more it hurts when you fall.

There are three things in this life you can be sure of: death, taxes, and more taxes.

Habits may not always be good for us, but they give us about the only permanence we can expect in this life.

Life is mostly just a matter of hanging on.

Life is a game that comes with no instructions, no time-outs, and only one rule: every move you make is final.

Life is a process of acquiring scar tissue.

Life is like a play: you don't really start to enjoy it until about the middle of the third act.

This is the future you gave things up for all your life.

Life is only as tough as you let yourself make it.

When life gets tough, the tough get a life.

Loaf and the world loafs with you; try and you try alone.

The lucky die young – it's the wise that get old and tired first.

Most mistakes are due to impatience.

Very few things in life are black or white – they're mostly just different shades of brown.

Life is a process of elimination – mostly on me.

Life may be short, but death is a whole lot shorter.

If life gave you enough time to get all of the information you needed to make a decision, you'd never be wrong. Of course you'd never get anything done, either.

It's not good food that makes a good meal; it's a good appetite.

Spring wouldn't be half as pretty is it didn't come right after winter.

The four stages of a man's life are raising hell, raising skirts, raising kids, and raising roses.

Trying to be like your kids may not be easy, but it's a lot easier than trying to make them be like you.

No matter how bad it gets, life is always preferable to its alternative.

Most folks will complain about their life right up to the point where they are about to lose it.

Since we are all going to die sooner or later, I guess about the best we can hope for is later.

Life is like a mystery novel: by the time you figure it out, it's almost over.

The only thing that's really worth a damn is life.

Life is a treadmill; if you're not getting ahead, you're dang sure falling behind.

Life isn't so much taking the time to smell the roses as it is taking the time to plant a few along the way.

Life is whatever the hell it takes.

The most important thing in the world is life, especially yours.

A man's life is the only thing he's got to enjoy. 'Seems to me he ought to spend more time on it than he does on other people's lives.

Being alive means being able to appreciate the uniqueness of every experience.

You only live now.

The only excuse for murder is murder.

Suicide ought to be a capital offense.

Life is about all a man can stand sometimes.

If life is the pits, this must be Indianapolis.

Life is like virginity: you don't think about it much until you're about to lose it.

Some folks say that life is too short, but I think life is long enough – it's only the weekends that are too short.

Lives may come and lives may go, but life stays pretty much the same.

Life is about winning.

If you're still alive, you're ahead.

Choose your companions carefully; we live our lives By imitation.

Life is like a round of golf. You've got to forget what you did on the last hole and concentrate on the one you're playing now.

A good life consists of good friends, good booze, and good sex.

You've got to live one day at a time. Just make sure it's today.

LOVE

I learned the meaning of love from my Mama and Daddy. If you ever saw those two together, you would know immediately there was nothing that could ever keep them apart. In spite of the occasional fussing and scrapping and sparring with each other – or maybe because of it – theirs was an affair that lasted through more than fifty years of depression and war, and death and disappointment, and sickness and poverty and drought. But it was always – at least from a child's point of view – an affair that radiated hope and warmth and love.

When I was very young, I equated love with fun – with the fun that lived in the brightness of Mama's smile and the warmth of Daddy's hug. Love was a pleasant sensation inseparably associated with the two most important people in my life. But as I grew older and began to experience love one-on-one, I came to realize that love is not always fun, or even pleasant, and that its source, far from being in the mercurial world about us, is deep within ourselves. The question of whether or not I could have come to that insight without my Daddy's guidance is moot.

You love people for what you are – not for what they are.

Love is just spoiling the hell out of each other.

Love, like charity, begins at home. You can't love somebody else if you don't like yourself.

The easiest place to find love is in another person.

Love makes the world go up and down.

When passion rules, reason abdicates.

Love is the only thing in the world that can make an old fool into a young fool.

Love is that powerful and wonderful magic that can make a toad out of a prince.

There aren't but two things can make a free man into a slave: love and ambition.

Love kept to itself turns to spite.

He who loves best lasts.

Love isn't something that man invented – it's something that women discovered.

The only thing that love has in common with justice is that they are both blind.

Love's harder on a man than it is on a woman.

The beginning of love may be lust, but the end of lust is love.

Love is that mysterious attraction that exists between any man and every woman.

Women fall in love – it grows on a man.

From the time you kiss your first girl, you're like a calendar: your days are numbered.

There are only two things that'll keep a man out of trouble: being in jail and the love of a good woman.

It's true that absence makes the heart grow fonder – of somebody else.

Love is demanding – mostly it demands money.

You can't buy love, but you can rent it pretty cheap.

Love and sex are like peas and pepper: peas may be kind of bland without a little pepper, but pepper without peas can be downright painful.

A man that loves everything loves nothing.

Hatred isn't the opposite of love – it's the absence of it.

'Fellow that loves everybody might make a good philanthropist, but he makes a dang poor husband.

It isn't love if she doesn't love you back.

Love unrequited turns to hatred – which is a lot easier for most folks to handle.

Love may be blind, but marriage is a real eye-opener.

Fortunately, being in love is a temporary affliction. Nobody could stand to listen to somebody talking about themselves like that for very long.

I'd rather be admired than loved, because admirers are more tolerant than lovers.

Love is what keeps a man up all night and down all day.

The secret of youth is love. If you love a woman enough to do everything she wants you to do, you won't have time to get old.

If you give somebody something without expecting something in return, that's not love – it's charity.

Charity doesn't care who gets it – it's given for the benefit of the giver, not the givee.

Love is giving somebody what you want.

Oh, what a tangled web we weave, when first we practice to conceive.

MANAGEMENT

I don't think Daddy ever managed anything bigger than a church baseball team, but he had acquired, either from astute observation and deduction or from desultory reading, a fairly accurate picture of what management ought to be – or at least what Daddy expected it to be. This vision was a pragmatic one, based on the perception of a personal need and honed by a propensity for perfection to a fine appreciation for the requisites of leadership. Daddy always felt that he had a right to expect superior performance not only from himself but, perhaps even more so, from those to whom he reported. That expectation – along with his readiness to decry his disappointment therein – was perhaps the determining factor in his having never achieved significant managerial status.

Yet one has trouble faulting him for failing to achieve what he obviously reproved, and his reproof of the institution of management as generally practiced is evident in the things he had to say about it. It was never Daddy's style, however, to be satisfied with complaining about a thing, and most of his observations, a few of which are recorded below, are couched in the instructive format with which those of us who knew him are so familiar.

A manager is somebody that knows how to get other people to do his work.

The more you trust people, the more you can.

A true craftsman takes care of the tools of his trade, and the tools of a manager's trade are his people.

A manager has got to know how to handle human beings, and that's usually easier if he happens to be one.

Manage and mandate are two different words.

The difference between a manager and an executive is the difference between a teacher and a preacher.

Responsibility means the ability to respond.

If you don't know what's going on, maybe it's you.

It's true that all men are lazy and opportunistic, but it is also true that they are all desperately hungry for recognition and appreciation and a feeling of belonging to and contributing to something bigger than they are. Now, if you feed that hunger, you won't have to stamp out laziness and opportunism – they will.

The first rule of management is take care of your people and they'll take care of you. The second rule is if you don't, they won't.

The most definitive feature of management is that they never seem to know what the hell's going on.

The greatest obstacle that any business has to overcome is management.

A manager has got to know two things: what's got to be done and how to make people want to do it.

A manager is like a coach: he's got to train his people, inspire them to win, and then let them.

A manager's job is to tell his people what he wants done – and to make sure they know how to do it.

If you don't speak Chinese, don't try to tell a Chinaman how to talk.

A manager is measured not by his methods but by his accomplishments.

Nobody really cares how you got the job done – or why you didn't.

The higher you get, the easier you are to get along without.

Activity is not the same thing as action.

Fixing the blame is not the same thing as fixing the problem.

Don't ask "who" unless your daughter is pregnant.

Ask not to whom the blame goes, it goes to thee.

Communication requires both talking and listening.

Managers who are always ranting about commitment ought to be committed.

A manager's main job is training, and there are only two reasons he could get in trouble: either he hasn't trained the people that report to him or he hasn't trained the people he reports to.

If you just go around bitching about enough things long enough, sooner or later you're bound to hit on something that really is wrong.

Management by committee is management by default.

Where I come from, most folks can't even *spell* committee.

You can't manage by – or on – the seat of your pants.

If what you want to do is sit at your desk and design systems, you'd better be working with computers, not people.

The only thing that scares people more than not knowing is knowing that you don't know.

If you have got to go out and kick a few asses, you have already failed as a manager.

There are three rules for effective management. The first is to always remember that everybody else is just like you are: selfish and uncaring; the second is to convince your people the *you* are *not* selfish and uncaring; and the third is to convince upper management that you *are* selfish and uncaring.

Team player is usually a euphemism for brown nose.

The trouble with most teams is that only yes men get on them.

No man can serve two masters, for either he will laugh at the one and tolerate the other, or he will tolerate the one and laugh at the other, depending on which one of them he's talking to at the time.

If the system doesn't work, work around the system.

The first to know are the first to go.

Accentuate a man's positives and *he* will eliminate his negatives.

The means is never the objective.

If you work with people long enough, you will find out two things: the first is that all people are basically the same and the second is that, in order to control them, you have first got to learn to control yourself. When you have discovered those two things, you will be a manager.

The mark of a good manager is that his people work harder when he's not there – 'cause they don't want to disappoint him.

An executive is like a blind man driving a team of horses: he can either give them their head and hope they don't turn the wagon over, or he can yank on the reins and make sure they do.

A manager is like a coach: he doesn't have to be able to run 90 yards for a touchdown, but he does have to know enough about the game to tell his players which way to run.

Learn before you lead.

Never believe what you read on bathroom walls or hear in staff meetings.

The mills of the gods grind slowly, but the gods don't have to bake bread for a living.

Plan in the morning and work in the afternoon – after everybody else has gone home.

Organization is mostly imposing your prejudices on other folks.

The purpose of organization is to cover your behind; things get done through disorganization.

The difference between Sales and Engineering:
- A Salesman will begin a presentation with a joke; an Engineer will begin a joke with a presentation.
- An Engineer will say, "That's a very aggressive adhesive"; a Salesman will say, "That is some sticky shit!"
- If a problem arises, a Salesman will try to save his account; an Engineer will try to save his ass.
- Engineers try to minimize costs; Salesmen try to maximize their expense accounts.
- Salesmen tell you what they think you want to hear; Engineers tell you what they think they know.

G. E. Kruckeberg

MARRIAGE

"I never been in too many institutions," Daddy used to say, "but from what I've heard about them, marriage has got to be the best of the lot."

My Daddy joked quite a bit about marriage – usually when Mama wasn't around – but I'm convinced that his levity on the subject was inspired solely by the expectations of the times. In an era dominated by radio renditions of the continual conflicts of Kingfish and Saphire and Fibber and Molly and the infamous Bickersons, a man's reputation as a wit depended to a great extent on his ability to lampoon the sacred institution of marriage.

That daddy took his institutionalization seriously, however, became apparent when Mama got sick. The sickness was one that was hard to diagnose, and after several doctors had erroneously proclaimed her difficulties to be psychosomatic, the family, including my wife at the time, turned against her. Ultimately, her problem was correctly diagnosed and surgically repaired, but the devotion and determination my Daddy displayed throughout that year and a half of need and rejection gave, for me at least, concrete meaning to the words: for better or for worse, in sickness and in health.

If this story of dedication seems inconsistent with the tenor of the quotations that follow, all I can say is that Daddy was the kind of guy that could laugh at the things he held most dear. Or maybe he just had to.

A man that doesn't drink or gamble has already got two strikes against him when it comes to domestic relations, because he's got nothing left to blame for his problems but his wife.

A woman never knows what kind of man she doesn't want until after she marries him.

The two most important days in a man's life are the day he gets his first car and the day he gets married – in that order.

A woman thinks sex is a part of marriage; a man thinks marriage is part of sex.

Marriage is love, honor, and oh boy!

The best way to keep a man from straying is to make sure he doesn't have any reason to.

If your best friend isn't your wife, it better be because you're single.

Marriage is supposed to culminate a love affair – not terminate it.

Marriages that spring from love affairs always seem to be healthier than those that develop from relationships.

In any household, everybody has got to march to the same drummer; in a happy household, the drummer is the woman of the house.

Marriage was invented by women, but they like to let men think it was their idea.

A woman gets security out of marriage – a man gets kids.

Most single men would rather be married, and most married men would rather be married to somebody else.

Variety is the spice of sex.

Sex is something that everybody needs – like food – but that doesn't mean you have to always eat in the same restaurant.

Nothing can motivate a man quicker than a wife.

The major difference between a woman and a man is that a woman really doesn't want to know where her spouse was until three o'clock in the morning.

The reason little girls are more carefree than little boys is that they know they will never have to put up with a wife.

I never complain – I got a wife to do that.

I never have a problem meeting expenses. My wife introduces me to them.

Women can afford to be optimistic, because they have made their husbands into pessimists.

Most women talk about twice as much as their husbands listen.

Women are victimized by their own self-importance – but not half so much as their husbands are.

A man can't be happy all the time – his wife won't let him.

Stupidity is picking an argument with your wife.

Whosoever taketh another man's wife by another man shall his wife be taken.

If marriage is not proof enough that cupid invented cupidity, divorce sure ought to be.

The perfect mate is the one you treat like one.

Marriage is a lot like life: it may not be perfect, but it's preferable to the alternative.

Women worry about the future 'til they get a husband; men never worry about the future 'til they get a wife.

A married man ought to forget his mistakes – there's no sense in two people remembering the same thing.

The secret to a happy marriage is two words: "yes" and "Ma'am."

When I was a young man, I was my own worst enemy – then I got married.

All men make mistakes – married men just pay more for theirs.

MATURITY

Where I grew up, one of the milestones of maturity for a boy was his first suit. I can still remember mine. It was a double breasted, garish brown herringbone with shoulder pads and cuffed and pleated trousers that flapped around my spindly legs when I walked. And it was beautiful.

The event that occasioned my acquiring this stunning piece of attire was my Sunday school graduation. In our church, Sunday school students who had attained the age of twelve by Palm Sunday were obliged to stand up in front of the congregation to receive a certificate of completion, a copy of the New Testament, and a handshake from Mr. Prochnau, the Sunday school teacher. They were then turned over to the pastor for a years instruction in the tenets of the church prior to their taking first communion the following Easter.

The graduation ceremony included a verbal examination, unrehearsed and conducted by Mr. Prochnau before the full body of the congregation. When my turn came, I stepped confidently up to the lectern. In my new suit, with my hair slicked down with Southern Rose and the snugness of one of Daddy's hand painted neckties secure about my throat, I felt ready for anything Mr. Prochnau might throw at me. I wasn't.

He asked me a geography question. Geography? Geography was my poorest subject in school! While I vaguely remembered hearing Mr. Prochnau talk about Tyre and Sidon, I must have been absent or daydreaming on the Sunday he told us which one of the two was an island. Well, what the heck. I had a fifty-fifty chance of guessing right, and in any case, guessing was the only choice I had.

I could tell from the look on Mr. Prochnau's face that I had guessed wrong.

Mr. Prochnau did a nice job of covering for me, and I got my certificate and Testament and handshake along with everyone else, but somehow I didn't feel I had achieved the level of maturity expected of me that day. Daddy apparently read my mood, because outside the church later, while Mama was taking a picture of us, he put his arm around my shoulder and said, "You know, son, maturity doesn't mean knowing a lot of things about the world – it means knowing a lot of things about yourself."

That was more than forty years ago, and I have yet to come across a better definition of maturity.

There's nothing in the world can change a man's attitude as much as a little maturity.

Maturity is mostly a matter of living long enough.

It's not how old you are that's important; it's how well you used the time.

Bad luck's easy to take, but a man needs a good deal of maturity to handle good luck.

Problems are the means of growth.

Maturity is what you get between your junior and your senior year.

Being mature helps you understand people better because you can remember back when you were young and dumb yourself.

You can tell a man that's mature from a man that's just old by whether or not he'd like to be young again.

You can't have maturity without a little age.

A man's old when he starts to think more about dying well than he does about living well.

When a man starts living in the past, he's getting old; when he stops living in the future, he*'s gotten* old.

No matter how old you are, mature is something that you are still getting.

A man is as old as his convictions.

Stability in a man is a sure sign of old age.

A man ought to have some respect for maturity – if only for his own.

The maturity of a culture is measured by the way they treat women; the maturity of a man is measured by the way women treat him.

Immaturity is its own reward.

Decline occurs only when it can no longer be ignored.

The reason that young folks think they know all of the answers is that they're not old enough yet to know what the questions are.

At the end of the banquet of life, old age is the dessert. It's the time that your kids, your appetite, and your sex drive all desert you.

The generation gap seems to be mostly between the ears.

A man's always got to be patient with younger men – maturity is still the only cure for stupidity.

Drivel is a sure sign of immaturity.

Maturity is when girls stop being a nuisance and become a necessity.

Ambition always seems to be strongest in the inexperienced.

A good son makes a good father.

You know you're grown up when you get yourself into a mess that your Daddy can't get you out of.

There are no old fools. Fools don't get to be old.

There's no tool like an old tool.

Cynicism is the cost of experience.

Grandkids give a man a second chance to be a good father.

If I'd known grandkids were going to be so dang much fun, I'd of had them first.

If God hadn't meant for kids to be spoiled, he wouldn't have given them grandparents.

Kids turn into adults when they become parents, and they turn into kids again when they become grandparents.

It's not easy being a kid – and it gets harder the older you get.

The only good thing about being grown up is that you get to act like a kid a lot.

It's not until you're old enough to know better that you get the opportunity.

Youth is the ability to enjoy.

The joys of youth become the regrets of age.

Getting old isn't so bad; it's not being young anymore that hurts.

A man raises roses when he can't raise anything else.

You're only as old as what you want to feel.

The most maturing experience any man will ever have is the death of his father.

As a man get older, he quits thinking about the quality of life and goes to thinking about the quantity.

The biggest problem with being old is that most folks don't know how to do it.

Just when a man reaches maturity, he starts getting senile.

Older doesn't necessarily mean smarter, but it sure as hell should.

Old folks who like to give good advice are usually just trying to make up for the bad examples they set when they were young.

Experience is spelled a-g-e.

The only thing more cruel than the honesty of old men is the honesty of young men.

Adults are children with bills.

Teenagers are children with hormones.

Tribulation is the price of maturity.

The thing that makes old men smarter than young men is the fear of death.

Beer won't give a man real maturity – but whiskey will.

The only problem with death is it leaves so dang many things undone.

Men don't get smart from being old; they get old from being smart.

Maturity is a bonus to the gift of parenthood.

Retirement is like an orgasm: the longer you can put it off, the better it is.

One nice thing about getting older is that sex takes Longer – 'course everything else does too.

Women age better than men – but then they looked a lot better than we did to start with.

THE MEDIA

We subscribed to both newspapers offered in our small town – the Republican morning paper and the Democratic evening paper – but other than during an election year, Daddy seldom read anything in either of them except the funny papers and "Believe It Or Not by Rippley." I can remember him listening to Edward R. Murrow and William Shirer and H. B. Kaltenborn on the radio during the war, but after 1945 he tended to eschew radio newscasts as a waste of time. When TV came along, Daddy confined his Saturday night viewing to *Gunsmoke* and *Have Gun Will Travel* and switched the set off when the ten o'clock news came on. In short, Daddy was a mediaphobe.

It wasn't that Daddy was against news. He would avidly devour each issue of *U. S. News and World Report*, a publication that he considered (after having gone trough subscriptions to both *Time* and *Newsweek*) to be the least biased source of news available at the time. His contention was not with information itself, but with the deliberate misinformation pandered by the newsmongers. "The only difference between TASS and the UP," he used to say in the early 'Seventies, "is that TASS is run by the 'ins.'"

Much of what follows was spoken by my Daddy during the divisive 'sixties and 'seventies – a time when many Americans were appalled by the specter of a free press run rampant – and although some of it may seem a bit theatrical more than twenty-five years after the fall of Saigon and fifteen years after the retirement of David Brinkley, I would urge the reader to keep in mind what my Daddy said: "The press is a beast that, under the Constitution, we can not control. Our only hope is to teach it to control itself."

157

All they want me to know is what I read in the newspapers.

"Truth" is what we call the propaganda that we print in *our* newspapers.

"Free press" means that they are free to print anything they want to; it doesn't mean it isn't going to cost you if you go and believe it.

"Truth in journalism" means what most folks will swallow, and the more folks that swallow it, the truer it is.

It's the job of the media to disseminate truth; identifying it is our job.

An honest man is the noblest work of some press agent.

Generally, newsmen have a pretty good vocabulary, but there are two words that most of them seem to be unfamiliar with: "truth" and "fairness."

Scandal is the stuff that circulation is made of.

Bad news makes good press.

Good news is no news.

Never tell a joke in front of a newsperson: either he will find a way to turn it into a racial slur or she will find a way to turn it into a sexual slur.

Strange bedfellows make politics newsworthy.

Newspapers only print what most folks want to believe.

The main difference between newspapers and graffiti is that newspapers are more obscene – and they have advertisements.

Mediocrity is the stuff they print in the media.

When I was a kid, we used to wrap garbage in newspapers. These days they come with it already in them.

The invention of the newspaper gave us disposable information. I guess from that point of view, television is an improvement.

For 450 years, the course of European history followed the writings of one man: Machiavelli. We'd all of been better off if he'd written in the newspapers.

Don't ever underestimate the power of the press; they beat the hell out of us in Viet Nam.

Wherever four newspaper columnists are gathered together, there's a fifth columnist in the midst of them.

In America, the fifth column is the fourth estate.

The trouble with newspapers these days is they got too dang many columunists.

The United States is the only country in the world that can boast that our newspapers lost us a war.

Most TV commentators I've seen would of done better if they'd gone into some other line of comedy.

American news media has progressed from Walter Winchell and Paul Harvey to hard-fought competition with the Disney channel.

I don't care much for TV. I've seen people die, and it's not something I want to watch for entertainment.

I never buy what I see on TV, especially if it's on a news program.

Don't ever trust pathological liars and news reporters.

Television is the biggest waste of time since getting drunk.

The function of the media seems to be to make sure that the doers and the diers don't ever get enough consistent information to reason why.

If folks who advertise had such a dang good deal, they wouldn't have to.

Don't believe anything that somebody's being paid to tell you.

You know a man's living in a world of illusion when all of his allusions are taken from television.

MORALITY

The human mind seems to have a propensity for remembering the unpleasant, a characteristic that has been extolled by some as a survival mechanism necessary to the preservation of the species. Be that as it may, I only know that there were precious few times in my young life that I didn't enjoy coming home from school, but the only ones I can remember are those few times that I didn't.

On one of those occasions, I had been guilty of fighting – an intolerable offense in a parochial school. There was no doubt that my parents were already aware of my infraction. The Principal had taken the trouble to telephone the news of my altercation on ahead of me – as though my bruised right eye and swollen lip wouldn't have been enough to condemn me in any case.

Daddy was waiting for me when I got home. As he led me to the fruit cellar, our equivalent of the proverbial woodshed, desperation fired my imagination. In hopes of deterring the inevitable, I began to explain to him how my belligerence had been inspired by a blatant affront to my dignity – the sort of insult that only a wimp could ignore.

"I understand," he said, after listening patiently, "but I don't condone everything I understand. Bend over."

There will always be good reasons for doing the wrong things.

Morality is something I hope I have got; conscience is something I hope everybody else has got.

161

Morality is the coin of the realm, but immorality is where the folding money is.

A man that counts his virtues is trying to hide his vices.

It may take all kinds, but *I* don't have to.

There is no right and wrong – there are just different ways of doing the same thing.

A belief is as true as it is useful.

Right is just a big word for expedient.

Morality isn't doing what other folks do; it's doing what other folks think you should do.

A man's either got to take the example of others or be used as an example to others.

The purpose of morality is not to please yourself, but to please the folks that could *keep* you from pleasing yourself.

Morality is what's best for everybody.

Christians didn't invent morality; morality invented Christianity.

I've only been accused of morality once in my life, and that was by a nearsighted agnostic.

Brevity is the soul of women's swimwear.

You can love your neighbor all you want – as long as you don't let your wife find out about it.

Moses just misunderstood: God didn't say sex was immoral – He said it was *immortal*.

Nobody sticks their nose into somebody else's business without the intention of doing them harm.

It's not the immorality of poverty that makes criminals – it's the immorality of wealth.

Vices sometimes turn out to be virtues in disguise – and virtues always turn out to be vices in disguise.

The most virtuous people are always among the greatest sinners.

Sin is just a big word for egocentricity.

The only real sin is laziness. All of the other ones come from it.

Morality is like the weather: if you don't like what it is today, wait awhile and it'll change.

If it weren't for immorality, a lot of folks wouldn't have anything at all to talk about.

It isn't a sin if nobody sees you doing it.

Money isn't the root of all evil – the belief that you deserve more of it is.

Everybody wants to be good, but some folks want to be good for nothing.

Rational means "good at rationalization."

PEOPLE

"There are a lot of things you don't have to understand to get along in this world," Daddy used to tell me, "But you have got to understand people, because you are one."

That admonition touches on an important part of my Daddy's philosophy: that people, in spite of whatever airs and pretenses they may affect, are still just people. From priest to prostitute and from skid row bum to megadollar-a-year CEO, we are all fellow occupants of the same, narrow evolutionary slot, and the better we understand and get along with each other, the better it will be for us and for all future generations of the race of mankind.

It should be evident from the quotations that follow that Daddy understood people. And more than that, he liked them, even though he knew they were not perfect. "People are seldom as good as they should be," he used to say, "but they're never as bad as they could be."

The less you expect from people the more you are going to be disappointed.

Some folks are born losers, but most of us have got to work at it.

The more you trust people, the more you can.

The only folks that aren't opportunists are those that are too lazy to put forth the effort.

The best way to learn to understand people is to learn to understand yourself.

Everybody's crazy – just over different things.

People don't react to what you do or what you say – they react to what they are.

A man's certainty varies inversely with his knowledge.

People are a lot like cats: they look smarter than they really are.

Everybody is ignorant; stupidity, however, requires extra effort.

The first thing you've got to remember about dealing with people is that they are just as scared as you are.

Man is the only animal whose ears close up whenever his mouth is open.

It's not so much that people believe what they want to believe, but that they want to believe what they believe.

Folks are always more ready to blame somebody else for their failures than they are for their successes.

Habit and instinct are what most folks call intelligence.

If people were half as good as they say they are, they'd be twice as good as they think they are.

Most people never do what they can because they never believed they could.

People are like dogs: they're real friendly one on one, but they start showing off as soon as they get in a pack.

Force is the first resort of the ignorant and the last resort of the lazy.

Folks that bore us are always easier to take than folks that are bored by us.

The only reason a man would draw your attention to somebody else's shortcomings is to draw your attention away from his.

I never met a man who didn't gripe.

The wheel that squeaks the loudest gets replaced.

Folks don't practice modesty much because it's the only virtue they can't brag about.

A man sees his own faults in others, but he always thinks his virtues are unique.

There are two kind of people: sinners who think they're not and non-sinners who think they are.

Virtue is in the eye of the virtuous.

Most folks would rather bad-mouth themselves than not talk about themselves at all.

Don't worry about what people will think. In most cases, what they think has more to do with what they think already than it does with anything you do or don't do.

Don't ever fool yourself into believing that you are dealing with rational people. You are always dealing with folks that are out to prove what they have already decided.

There are four kinds of people: warriors, merchants, priests, and peasants. The first three have been responsible for all of human progress – and for most of human misery.

There's only one thing people are more scared of than change, and that's changing back and forth.

It seems the more alike folks are, the harder they look for differences to fight about.

Creative people read the funny papers.

An optimist says, "I've only got halfway to go." A pessimist says, "I'm only halfway there."

The meanest people are always the nicest people.

I like books better than people, because books don't borrow people and not bring them back.

Man is the only animal that knows he's going to die, and I think maybe that's why he developed such an ability to ignore the inevitable.

If it weren't for people, a man wouldn't have anything to worry about.

A man's got to be right at least eighty percent of the time, because at least eighty percent of the people would rather remember the twenty percent of the time he was wrong.

There are two kinds of people: those who divide the world up into two kinds of people and those who don't.

Never try to make a fool out of a man – he can always do a better job of it himself.

People work together only because proximity makes it easier for them to work against each other.

People never notice how you react to them; they're always too busy reacting to themselves.

Most folks see what they're looking for, not what they're looking at.

The only thing that most people really need is a little encouragement.

The beginning of wisdom is the realization that all men are *not* created equal.

Be an observer of people; it does wonders for your self-esteem.

All human action is reaction, and most human action is a reaction to something that happened a long time ago.

The smaller the man, the bigger the truck he drives.

PERSISTENCE

My Daddy never said much about persistence – mainly because he didn't call it that. He called it grit, and grit was what he exhorted my brother and me to develop and what, we were given to understand, was the major component in a man's resistance to being "ground down" by the trials and tribulations of life. Grit was a quality that we were expected to display at work and at school and at play. It meant a lot of things, but mostly it meant just going on without complaining.

The most exemplary display of grit I've ever seen was the time Daddy hit himself in the head with an eight pound sledge. The woodpile was at the back of the yard, just past where Mama's clothesline was strung. Daddy was splitting wood with his back to the house, and as he brought the hammer back over his head, he inadvertently hooked it on the clothesline behind him. At the precise instant that the sledge met the wedge, Daddy's wrists refused to resist the elastic energy his arms had imparted to that clothesline, and the head of the hammer snapped back and caught him right between the eyes. He went to his knees. I thought he was dead. But there was no blood – just a dazed look in his eyes as he staggered to his feet, walked over to the clothesline post, took out his pocket knife, and cut the clothesline. Then he walked back, picked up his sledge, and went back to splitting wood.

Lesser men might have malingered or complained. They might have gone in the house to listen to the radio and nurse the bruise on their forehead for the rest of the day, or they might first have maligned their wives for having left a damn clothesline in their way and *then* gone in the house to listen to the radio and nurse the bruise on their forehead. But Daddy had wood to split, and he had grit.

You haven't lost until you quit.

Persistence is something you admire in everybody else and can't stand in your kids.

A man will give up what he's got quicker'n he'll give up what he wants.

Persistence is just making a nuisance of yourself.

The best idea in the world won't work – unless you do.

If you don't hang in, somebody's dang sure gonna hang you out.

Persistence in your friends is the same thing as stubbornness in your enemies.

Ninety percent of your failures could have been successes with just one more try. The other ten percent might have taken two.

If you feel like giving up on something, give up on quitting.

History always gets written by the winners.

Survivors are people who are too scared, too lazy, or too dumb to quit.

Persistence is the glue of success.

You can't hit it if you don't swing at it.

Most folks'll step aside for any man that looks like he won't.

The problem is never the first thing you find wrong.

It takes more than one sore muscle to make a horse go lame.

Beware the simple solution, because there are no simple problems.

Simple solutions appeal to simple people.

Just because it's obvious doesn't mean it's already been tried.

Trying the same thing over and over is perversion, not persistence.

Habit is a caricature of persistence.

Don't draw if you're not gonna shoot.

It's not easy being right, especially when you're the only one that is.

Giving in doesn't always mean giving up.

The nice thing about persistence is it doesn't require a man to think much.

Horses and people both follow carrots on sticks; the difference is that horses get tired of it after awhile.

If at first you don't succeed, blame it on someone else.

Nothing is impossible – so long as you are not the one that's got to do it.

Chess teaches persistence, because that's what it takes to find somebody else crazy enough to play the game with you.

The only thing worse than losing is quitting.

You're better off being persistent than lucky, 'cause luck comes in two kinds: good and bad.

POLITICS

For men of my Daddy's vintage, politics was a second profession. It was the thing men talked about – and often argued about – in barber shops and auction barns and bars.

These were men who had weathered the Depression and withstood the hardships of World War II – men who took their politics seriously, and for whom the workings of the government in Washington were a matter of personal concern, to be watched and debated. It was not uncommon for a man of that era to be exalted by his peers more for his understanding of politics than for his understanding of women.

I'm afraid Daddy was not rated highly in at least the first of these areas of expertise among the men of his time. Although political discussions were normally restricted to adult males, I chanced to be present as a silent observer at enough of them as I was growing up to realize that my Daddy was considered to be a middle-of-the-road Democrat – the kind of man who might even vote a split ticket!

At a time when politics was widely perceived to be the major source of solutions, Daddy tended to view it as part of the problem. He had the sometimes-irritating habit of looking past the politicians and the issues and concentrating on the weaknesses and faults of the political system – a system that, as one can see from the quotations that follow, both fascinated and frightened him. But it always amused him.

Politics is the art of convincing the middle-of-the-road majority that your crazy ideas are less dangerous than the opposition's crazy ideas.

The funny thing about politics is the politicians.

There're only two things in this world I'm scared of: tornadoes and politicians.

Anybody that can make a living at politics has got to be doing *something* wrong.

Ask not what your country can do for you; ask what your country is doing *to* you.

Politics and honesty go together like snakes and women.

The common denominator in America is politics – it's the one thing that divides us all.

What a politician says isn't what he believes; it's what he wants *you* to believe.

When a politician points to something with pride, he most likely had nothing to do with it; and when he views something with alarm, he's more than likely responsible for it.

An honest man is the noblest work of his press agent.

It may be true that you can draw flies with honey, but who wants lumpy honey?

People aren't so much interested in politics as they are in government.

Politics is the religion of the strong.

Politics is the organization of discontent.

The only thing in God's creation lower than a politician is a political activist.

If you still think Joe McCarthy was wrong, look at how many men have died in Viet Nam because of Hollywood politics.

. E. Kruckeberg

The three lowest professions in the world are politician, pimp, and rapist-murderer – in ascending order.

There are no honest politicians; it's just that some of them are more dishonest than others.

The difference between a politician and a prostitute is a politician sells what doesn't belong to him.

In politics, the common denominator is common greed.

The most disgusting thing about politicians is all them strange bedfellows they make.

There aren't but two choices in American politics: the thieves or the scoundrels.

The only good thing about an election is that one of them rascals has got to lose.

Whoever wins the election, it won't be the electorate.

Liberalism is a mental disorder in which the sufferer feels responsible for all of the problems in the world.

There are no liberal atheists; to be a liberal, you have got to believe that God gave you the right to change the laws of economics.

A liberal is a radical with money.

The only people who can afford to be liberal are those with a lot of money in their bank accounts – or very little in their constituencies.

The thing I don't like about Liberals is they want to be liberal with *my* money.

Liberalism always seems to end up with more poor people than it started with. I guess that's because the liberal politicians have got to keep inventing them.

The only sensible thing that Democrats ever talk about is Republicans.

A conservative is anyone whose interests are at stake.

The Democratic principle is feed the needy and squeeze the greedy.

The New Deal wouldn't of been such a bad deal is they hadn't used the same old deck.

Folks in Washington seem to think that *Laisez Faire* means that we are supposed to leave *them* alone.

There aren't but two reasons a fellow would want to take your guns away: either he's planning to do something to you or he's afraid you're gonna find out about something he's already *done* to you.

Immobility is not the same thing as stability.

Passing legislation is a lot like passing gas: the quieter you are about it, the easier it is to blame it on somebody else.

Passing laws usually solves problems only for out of work lawyers.

Materialism may have a bad name in some circles, but it does pay the bills.

The only thing anybody ever got for nothing was nothing.

Equality appeals only to inferior people.

Opportunity is a better cure for poverty that equality.

Democracy won't work as long as most folks want to be told what to do.

People only fight wars; it takes a government to make one.

Clausewitz had it backwards. War's not an act of politics; politics is an act of war.

War is not natural to man, but it is to politics.

"Give me liberty or give me death" was spoken by a politician, not a soldier.

Wars are like babies; it takes two to make one.

Wars are made by old men – and lost by young ones.

Old soldiers never die; they're behind the lines – running Supply.

If war isn't hell, the devil missed a good bet.

Folks in the South are funny; they talk Republican and vote Democrat.

There are three sides to every question: the radicals on one side, the radicals on the other side, and the majority in the middle who don't give a damn one way or the other.

The middle of the road is where the yellow stripe is.

Most of the road kill is either to the right or the left of the middle of the road.

The mills of the gods don't grind near as slowly as the mills of the government.

Politics is the oil of society.

The business of politics is to iron out differences, not to teach religion. Religion is the *cause* of the differences.

The only problem with government is politics.

The main reason it's so hard to communicate with politicians is that they are always listening to themselves.

Politician is spelled p-a-r-a-s-i-t-e.

Terrorism is political masturbation: it might make the terrorist feel good, but the only offspring is disgust.

PREJUDICE

"I had a deprived childhood," Daddy used to say. "When I was growing up, there weren't but two kinds of people around here: German Lutherans and German Catholics. And since the Catholics were too dang nice to hate, I grew up not having anybody to hate at all."

Whether that alleged deprivation was a contributing factor or not, Daddy did seem to have very few prejudices where people were concerned. He was always extremely tolerant of anything a man couldn't help, and except for sexual deviation or outright criminal activity, he was moderately tolerant of a lot of things a man could help.

This is not to imply, you understand, that he wasn't prejudiced. He was. Daddy had very definite and adamant views on a great number of things – cars, for instance.

When I was growing up, you could go from Chevy country to Ford country by driving twenty miles down the highway to the next town. The predominance of one or the other of the Big Two in any locale was a function of its dominant dealership, and one of the major businesses in the town where I grew up was Bauer Chevrolet. Consequently, along with nearly everybody else in town, Daddy was a Chevy man. "The fear of the Ford is the beginning of wisdom," he always said. In our household, we referred to cars we used to have not by model, but simply by year – the '28, the '37, the '41, etc. They had all been Chevrolets.

You can imagine my surprise then when I got out of the Navy and Mama and Daddy and my Brother drove out to California to pick me up in a fire-engine red '54 Ford station wagon. After all the hugs and handshakes were over, I asked Daddy how he liked the Ford.

"It was your Mama's idea," he said. "She kinda liked it."

"But how do you like it?" I persisted.

"Well," he said, "it's sorta like moonshine whiskey – it's good, but you're ashamed of it."

Prejudice is anything you do to somebody who accuses you of doing it because of prejudice.

I don't have anything against Christianity. I dislike all religions equally.

Discrimination is the first mark of intelligence.

A man can afford to be tolerant only outside of his own family.

Tolerance is not the same thing as approval.

There's no sense worrying about a man's creed or color – if he's a man, he can't get any worse than what he already is.

Segregation is as much as a man can afford.

Tolerance is ignoring what you don't give a damn about anyhow.

What a thing is worth is always determined by prejudice.

What most folks mean by rationality is what conforms to their prejudices.

Bias is almost always economically motivated.

Prejudice doesn't happen without a reason.

Don't begrudge a man music just because you can't dance.

The best way to make sure a kid ends up bad is to keep on telling him how good he is.

Bussing is just a plot by the school bus manufacturers to sell more busses.

You can't stamp out segregation by segregating folks.

Intolerance is ten percent prejudice and ninety percent ignorance.

The only thing more intolerant than the worst bigot is the most tolerant religion.

Politicians tend to talk a lot about equality, mainly because you don't get a lot of votes acting superior or calling other folks inferior.

Biased means being an ass twice: once for screwing up and once for trying to blame somebody else.

Out of the mouths of babes comes mostly what we put in them.

Where bigotry is bliss, 'tis folly to be fair.

Minority problems eventually solve themselves because minorities always have higher birth rates.

You're not gonna keep a dog from barking by telling him he's a cat.

Prejudice is a subconscious estimation of probability.

Prejudice is making decisions without taking the time to think about them.

Where I come from, if you got more than two kids, everybody thinks you're Catholic.

Intolerance is the last resort of the incompetent.

Intolerance is caused by environmental deficiencies – mostly those of the intolerant.

Don't blame your weaknesses on other folks' strengths.

The cost of segregation is ignorance.

The only people who are totally free of prejudice and intolerance are hypocrites.

Generalizations are always safe. It's applying them that gets you into trouble.

Organization is mostly imposing your prejudices on other folks.

Hatred is a disease peculiar to the inferior.

Prejudice is a survival mechanism.

If you're fighting yesterday's battles, you're losing today's.

PRINCIPLE

"A man of principle," Daddy used to say, "is a man that follows somebody else's rules."

Although that definition might at first glance seem to be an attempt to disparage conformity, I can assure you that that was not my Daddy's intent. On the contrary, he was echoing, albeit unconsciously, Rousseau's famous dictum that individual freedom is the price of civil liberty – that a man has to give up freedom of choice on one level to gain freedom of choice on another. Daddy was very much aware that he owed his individual freedom – as we all do – to an individual commitment to protect the individual freedom of everybody else. Following the rules, to Daddy's way of thinking, was one of the ways a man of principle kept up his end of that bargain.

Yet he was aware that the rules were variable, and that some principles were better or worse than others. He had even had some personal experiences that convinced him that some so-called principles are downright counterproductive. Still, a man of principle followed the rules, however hard he might work to change them. The only alternative, as Daddy saw it, was chaos and anarchy. Besides, as he always said, "A man without principles is a man with only one direction – jail."

It's easier to fight for a principle than it is to live by one.

A man is his principles.

G. E. Kruckeberg

Good principles don't make up for bad theory.

Sticking by their principles is some folks' principal principle.

Principle is usually an excuse for not doing something – or for doing something wrong.

Some folks seem to think that sticking to your principles is more important than what they are.

Principle is something folks talk about only when they run out of other folks to talk about.

Everybody's got principles – they just don't all agree with mine.

The right is always a minority.

'Fellow that says "it's the principle of the thing" is usually trying to justify what he knows is wrong.

In the real world, there is only one principle: if it works, let it; if it doesn't, forget it.

The only people that have time to worry about the principle of the thing are those that aren't involved in the doing of the thing.

A belief is as true as it is useful.

The only useful principle is the pragmatic principle: the means justify the ends.

Principles and getting things done are natural enemies.

Principles are something for old men to argue about.

Most folks aren't so much interested in the principle of the thing as they are in the cost of the thing.

It's not the principle of the thing that bothers me so much as it is the danged interest.

If a fellow tells you he's a man of principle, he isn't.

182

Principles are about the only things that poor people have to cherish.

The only principle I've got a problem with is the one that says I have got to accept other folks' principles.

A man without principles is like a horse without a bridle.

Whatever principles a man might have are better than having none at all.

A principle is like a god: some folks worship it to control others, some folks worship it to control themselves, and most folks worship it out of habit.

Principles are nice things to have – if you can afford 'em.

First principles always come from second thoughts.

'Fellow that says "it oughta work accordin' to principle" usually hasn't got the principle down real good.

The difference between principles and basics is usually about 150 pages and fifteen dollars.

Principles are things that only poor people can afford.

The principle of cause and effect says that every effect becomes the cause of an equal and opposite effect; I guess that's why folks are always going around in circles.

The principle of evolution says that ability is always proportional to demand, but it would be nice if it were equal to it once in a while.

The first principle of thermodynamics says that in any system, efficiency is always as high as it can get. Too bad that principle doesn't apply to the government.

Self-aggrandizement is the first principle.

A principle is a poor excuse for not thinking.

The first principle of finance is forget the principal – it's the interest that counts.

The first principle of education is never get sent to the Principal's office.

'Fella that says he has never compromised his principles probably never had any.

PROCRASTINATION

Never let it be said that my Daddy didn't know the meaning of the word procrastination. I was there the day he learned it.

It was a Sunday afternoon in July. The glare of the summer sun made things outside the soothing shade under the willow tree's low-hanging branches seem timeless and surreal, and the mid-day silence was disturbed only by the buzzing of bumblebees and the far off crooning of a turtle dove. Daddy, still wearing the slacks and undershirt he'd worn to church that morning, was stretched out in a hammock, dozing fitfully over a sea of German Benz grass that was on the verge of going to seed.

Mama had just finished washing the dishes after one of her typically fabulous Sunday dinners, and as she walked out onto the back porch, the slam of the screen door augured her mood.

"Ed," she yelled. "You promised coming home from church you were going to cut the grass today, and there you are sleeping the day away. You're nothing but a dang procrastinator."

Daddy, obviously startled, bolted up out of that hammock blithering, "Honey, I swear to God, I ain't never procrastinated with anybody but you." By the time Mama stopped laughing, Daddy had got the whole front yard and half of the back mowed.

Procrastination is the fear of failure.

Never put off 'til tomorrow what you can put off 'til next week.

185

Nobody ever got any medals for something they didn't do.

It always costs more to put it off than it does to just go ahead and do it.

The main reason folks keep putting stuff off until tomorrow is they've got to do today what they put off yesterday.

The right man for the job is the one that'll get around to doing it.

A thing worth doing is a thing that's worth more the quicker you get it done.

Anything can be replaced – except time.

The best cure for procrastination is to start.

The more you do, the more you can.

There are two kinds of people in the world: wishers and doers.

You'll never get anything done if you don't expect to.

Religion is the handmaiden of procrastination.

Putting a thing off comes of putting a higher priority on something else; procrastination comes of putting a higher priority on anything else.

The quicker you do something, the quicker you're going to have to do it again.

The longer you procrastinate, the easier it gets.

People always notice the things you *didn't* get done.

Not doing it on time is the first step toward not doing it at all.

Putting something off isn't so bad – it's when you *keep* putting it off that you got a problem.

Don't worry about what you didn't get done. Compliment yourself on what you didn't put off.

Tomorrow's another day – and another opportunity to procrastinate.

Most folks would procrastinate more if they didn't keep putting it off until it was too late.

A man won't do anything he doesn't have to.

Most folks wouldn't procrastinate so much if they knew more about what they were supposed to be doing.

Putting off is the same thing as giving up.

Procrastinators put it off longer.

There are three basic rules for teaching people to procrastinate:
1. focus on their failures,
2. ignore their accomplishments, and
3. belittle their abilities.

Procrastination is like lightning – it only occurs under low-pressure conditions.

The decision to procrastinate is one that every man makes for himself.

There's only one person you can blame for your procrastination – and you can do it all by yourself.

Procrastination and prevarication are Siamese twins.

Don't put off more than you can put over.

Never put off what you can't put back.

Putting a man off is the same thing as putting him down.

Waste makes haste.

Nobody wants to put up with a fellow that's always putting things off.

Putting off comes of being scared of putting forth.

A man always spends more time not doing than he does doing.

PROGRESS

Daddy was born in 1909 – the same year Peary reached the North Pole. Only one year earlier, Ford had introduced the Model T, and five years before that, the Wright brothers had flown the first airplane at Kitty Hawk, North Carolina. Daddy was three years old when one of the biggest ocean liner ever built went to the bottom of the North Atlantic on her maiden voyage, and he was five years old when the Panama Canal opened. My Daddy was a child of the progressive era – an era of giant accomplishments and giant expectations – and he grew up believing that progress was not only the primary goal of civilization but the sole salvation of mankind. When he was eighteen years old, he learned to fly Curtis Jennies, and when he was nineteen, he bought a brand new 1928 Auburn automobile – just twenty months before the progressive dream faltered in the stock market crash of October 1929.

My Daddy's generation never totally recovered from the thirties. Even during the postwar boom years, progress was fettered by the general fear of recurrent economic failure. It was as though, having seen both the up side and the down side of progress, they had developed a resistance to euphoria. That resistance is evident in some of the things Daddy had to say about progress.

Progress is a verb, not a noun.

It's not being best but getting better that counts.

G. E. Kruckeberg

Progress is the process of turning failure into success.

The only thing standing in the way of progress is prosperity.

Discontent is the father of change.

Progress is something you make, not something you wait for to happen.

You can't have growth without progress.

It's not progress if it's not getting better.

A lot of folks see progress in just changing styles.

Sometimes the road to progress runs backwards.

The only way you can whistle in the wind is to turn your back to it.

You can't stop change. The best you can do is try to use it to your advantage.

Habit is the biggest enemy of progress.

We don't progress in a straight line; we progress by going around in circles.

The only real inventions of mankind are religion and murder.

Progress has always run athwart of religion – if you got the only answer, any other attempt to improve the human condition has got to be blasphemy.

You can't have progress without defying a little authority.

The only reason a sane man would take a risk is that he's hoping to gain more than he's risking.

The father of progress may be passion, but it's mother is persistence.

190

There's a whole lot of human progress been achieved by students who weren't paying attention when their professors told them it couldn't be done.

You can't have progress until folks are ready for it.

"Fulton's Folly" was an epithet invented by sail makers.

You can't have harmony and progress at the same time.

It's easier to take off against the wind.

The greatest restraint on progress is procrastination, and the father of procrastination is fear.

Nothing makes the time pass more quickly than thinking about the future.

A thing being "in progress" is not the same as a thing progressing.

The most civilizing event in recent history was the invention of the automobile, because nothing makes a man more uncivilized than having to deal with horses and mules.

America's like the weather: what's in the East is history; you've got to look to the West to see the future.

We live in the future; we only plan in the present.

Labor unions are the biggest impediment to progress since religion.

The South's gonna rise again – from the ashes of the unions.

REGRET

My Uncle Harry rode a motorcycle – a pastime certain to instill admiration in the mind of any boy – and the aromas of cigarette smoke and whiskey that always hung about him conjured up visions of adventure and daring to equal that of the characters in "Terry and the Pirates." On the rare occasions he and Daddy took me fishing with them, Uncle Harry would always bring extras of his famous ham sandwiches for me, and he was ever solicitous of my well-being, except when he'd had too much to drink – which was often.

I knew Uncle Harry had a tragic past – I'd heard Mama talking about how he'd lost his first wife in childbirth, and how he blamed himself because he had left her alone that night to go out drinking with friends – but that aura of tragedy only added to his mystique in my young eyes.

Uncle Harry painted cars for a living, and he died before his time. The doctors said his lungs were eaten away. I remember standing by his grave with Daddy beside me, thinking of how much I was going to miss him, and hearing myself saying, "Uncle Harry wasn't really very happy, was he Daddy?"

"No, he wasn't," Daddy said. Then, as if suddenly realizing why I'd asked the question, he looked down at me and said, "Y'know, son, a man can't live without having some regrets. But he's a damn fool to keep 'em."

The major cause of disappointment is expectation.

Success is not having any regrets.

Don't regret your mistakes unless you didn't learn anything from them.

Regret's what keeps old maids and drunks from getting married and sober.

Regretting something you've already done is like wishing for something you've already got.

Men regret their weaknesses more than their crimes.

A clear conscience is a sure sign of a cloudy memory.

Regret is supposed to keep a man from doing the same thing again, not keep him from doing anything at all.

The only thing I've ever regretted is not discovering girls sooner than I did.

If a man knew he was gonna regret something before he did it, he'd be a damn fool to do it; and if he didn't know, he's a damn fool to regret it.

Regret is the ultimate masochism.

Knowing he's wrong will make a man mad quicker than anything else.

Regret never changed the past, but it sure can change the future – for the worse.

The only thing less productive than worrying about the future is regretting the past.

Regret is for the dead – the living require hope.

Worry and regret are the twin offspring of indecision.

"Might have been" is a dream of the past. The future starts from "wasn't."

The only man that's got no regrets is a liar.

193

The trouble with regret is it's always too late.

It's better to regret doing something than to regret not having done it.

Don't waste time feeling sorry for what you did. If you'd had any choice, you wouldn't have done it.

Regret is a sure sign of old age.

A man that's regretting the past isn't planning for the future.

Resolve is the best of masters; regret isn't even a good companion.

It's better to forget than to regret.

Regretting something you couldn't help is like blaming somebody for something they didn't do.

Regret's a bigger waste of time than television.

There are no small regrets – unless they're somebody else's.

Big people generally have little regrets, and big regrets are a sure sign of little people.

A man's better off doing nothing than something he'll have to apologize for.

The best way to keep from regretting your mistakes is to laugh at them.

If I had my life to live over, there are a lot of mistakes I'd have made sooner.

RELIGION

My Daddy was born German Lutheran, graduated from a parochial school, and was confirmed in the Lutheran church. He was, at different times, both an usher and a deacon, and except during deer season, he could be found in church nearly every Sunday morning. But I can't remember ever hearing him say, "I'm going to church." He always said, "I'm taking your Mama to church."

While Daddy was certainly what most people would call a good Christian (by which they mean someone who goes to church) and his natural philanthropy led most people to believe that he was an active Christian, the truth is that Daddy was not what most people would call religious. He was by no means an atheist, or even an agnostic. His argument was not with God but with the human institution of religion. Daddy was convinced that the church was not only unnecessary to a man's salvation, but that some of it's precepts and practices might actually handicap his progress toward that goal.

But Mama was religious, and Daddy took her to church on Sundays. That left him only one outlet for his true feelings on the subject, a few of which I've recorded below.

Intelligence is the only thing that separates man from the animals — and from religion.

The worse thing religion ever did to us was teach us to measure differences on a scale of right and wrong.

Religion is popular among lazy people, because the only other way they can get to be better than their neighbor is to work harder than he does.

There are two ways to get ahead: work hard, and work hard and pray.

The more backward a country is, the more religious it seems to be. Or maybe it's the other way around.

If you want to see what religion can do to improve the fellowship of mankind, take a good look at the Arabs.

Religion is a game for the weak; the strong play politics.

The purpose of religion is to legitimize our atrocities.

To swear is human.

The trouble with resisting temptation is you never know for sure that you're going to get a second chance.

God must love Christians – He made them so much like their own image of Him.

Christians love sinners; it's each other they can't stand.

'Fellow wouldn't have near so many faults if he didn't have so many Christians around to point 'em out to him.

Never trust a Christian – or anybody else that's got just one answer for everything.

I don't have anything against Christianity – I dislike all religions equally.

Mass is the opiate of the religious.

Real Protestants protest against all religions.

Of all the religious symbols I've ever seen, I think the fish is the most appropriate.

The fact that most people seem to be in more of a hurry to get to work on Monday morning that they were to get to church on Sunday ought to tell you something about the popularity of religion.

I figure if a man thinks he needs to go to church, he probably does.

The only thing more dangerous than a wise man is a good man.

Saints are just reformed sinners.

The fellow that admits to having little faults is just trying to direct your attention away from his big ones.

I don't mind tribulation; what I do mind is folks telling me it's good for me.

If God chastises only those he loves, that right there ought to be enough to make a man an atheist.

There aren't but two reasons a man would lie to you: either he's trying to cheat you or he's a preacher.

The greatest sinners make the best preachers.

When a preacher says he wants to share something with you, it generally turns out to be something of yours.

Religion was invented by priests – not the other way around.

I'm not in the habit of paying preachers for the privilege of working for 'em.

Going to church doesn't make a man a Christian any more than going to a stable makes him a horse.

If God *was* a woman, it sure would explain a lot.

Heaven would be a lot more desirable place if a fellow didn't have to die to get there.

Living on earth is just about all the heaven a man needs. If there is a heaven after death, it's just frosting on the cake.

I reckon praying doesn't hurt much, so long as you don't try to tell God what to do and how you want it done.

You'll generally get things quicker working for them than you will praying for them.

Faith is what you've got to have when you don't have much self-confidence.

The biggest problem with Protestants is that they don't have to go to confession.

Man has always invented religions – mostly to protect himself from other religions.

Religion has always been the source of its own destruction: education.

To religion, a little knowledge really *is* dangerous.

If religion is perfect, why does a man need to practice it?

Religion is a euphemism for hypocrisy.

Religion is the ultimate excuse.

The biggest problem philosophers have got is to come up with a reason for people to cooperate as strong as the one offered by religion.

The driving force in the building of 19th Century America wasn't the Carnegies and the Rockefellers – it was small town Protestants.

The faith of our fathers was in themselves.

Nothing in the world can fragment people like a little religion.

The really great anarchists were all in a pulpit.

Religion works – it just doesn't accomplish a whole lot.

Thank God for Christians – if it weren't for them, we'd have only one-day weekends.

Preacher is spelled p-a-r-a-s-i-t-e.

Religious freedom is an oxymoron – all religions abhor freedom of any kind.

The greatest revolution in history was the Protestant Revolution, 'cause it taught men to think for themselves.

The Industrial Revolution was the offspring of the Protestant Revolution.

Separation of Church and State is the only way to preserve the State.

REPARTEE

I don't know if Daddy knew what repartee meant, but I know he was good at it. I remember standing patiently beside him one Sunday morning after church and listening to the congregation's biggest busybody haranguing Mama. While her three ill-bred and undisciplined children were stomping through flower beds, trying to climb the flagpole, and generally disrupting the peace and sanctity of the Sabbath, the woman went on and on about the fact that Sally Smart was pregnant and didn't Mama think that was terrible since Sally's Daddy had been committed to an asylum for the last eight years and everybody knew her Granddaddy had been an eccentric old coot who had once set fire to the County Courthouse just because the Sheriff had beat him at a game of dominoes and what did Mama think ought to be done about it?

After two or three minutes of this drivel, Daddy cleared his throat and said, "Emma, I just don't see how you can suggest that insanity is hereditary. Hell, most folks around here get it from your kids."

To a disgruntled customer: We aim to please; we're just not sharpshooters.

To the response, "How'd you know that?": You mean everybody doesn't?

To a suggestion that he was engaged in a menial task: There are no menial tasks – just menial people.

To my Cousin when she was bragging about her boyfriend: Well, Honey, if he's so dang smart, how come he hung the moon crooked?

To Grandma when she defended her fussing and fretting as "mother love": Mom, I think you left the "s" off the front of that word.

To someone belaboring the cuteness of a baby: All babies are cute; if they weren't, adults would kill 'em.

To someone who accused him of lacking sensitivity: Sensitivities are like tits: everybody's born with them, but they just never develop in men.

To someone who told him that most automobile accidents occur within five miles from home: 'You suggesting I park five miles from the house and walk back and forth?

To someone who insisted that nothing is impossible: OK, let me see you bite your teeth.

To someone who insisted that he always told the truth: Mister, if you *knew* the truth, you wouldn't have the courage to tell it.

To someone who accused him of having bad habits: A habit's only bad if it's not one of mine.

To someone who asked him why he drank brandy: 'Cause folks think you're a lush if you drink whiskey straight.

To Mama when she accused him of forgetting something: Honey, I didn't forget, I just didn't remember.

To a friend who accused him of being forgetful: Shoot! I got a memory like a...uh...whatta you call them big gray things with long noses?

To a woman who was bemoaning the fate of the American Indian: Ma'am, the Indians got the same problem as the South: they lost.

To a man with whom he was riding into town one morning: John, you keep fighting traffic like this, your wife's gonna be a war widow.

To a man who was complaining about his bad luck: I don't know what the thunder you done, but it sounds to me like you better go to confession.

To a young woman who was shining up to him in a bar: Honey, I think you're barking up the wrong he.

To someone who commented on his talking to himself: Well, I'm one of the few people around here who's intelligent enough to understand what I'm saying, but I must say you're in the majority.

To an overconfident and flippant young man: Boy, I'm old enough to be your father – and a hell of a lot smarter.

To the question, "What hobbies do you have?": Just my wife. She's the only one I can afford.

To the question, "You got it?": Yeah, I got it. I just don't know what to take for it.

In response to the phrase "untimely demise": Every demise is untimely to the demisee.

To an old enemy who asked him for a hand: The only way I'd give you a hand would be rolled up.

To a surly waiter: Yeah, I'll give you a tip: don't get in an argument with a man that just lost his job and his wife in the same day.

To a flippant clerk in a small town store: I never could understand how a one-horse town can have so damn many horse's asses in it.

To a union organizer: Job security, hell! If you want job security, go get a job as a Ford mechanic.

To a lazy employee: If you think you deserve a break today, go get a job at McDonalds.

To the question, "Who you gonna believe, him or me?": Well, I generally believe the fellow that doesn't feel he has to ask that question.

To the comment, "Enjoy it while you can. Tomorrow may never get here.": Yeah, it might not. But what if it does?

To a chronic embellisher: If you were Catholic, you'd have to say so many Hail Marys for lying you'd have to take a four day leave of absence twice a week.

To Mama when she showed him something she'd bought at a garage sale: I think you left the "b" out of the middle of that word, didn't you, Honey?

Of a friend of Mama's who affected a nautical air: The only sailing she's ever done is garage saleing.

To someone who accused him of being ambivalent: Well now, I just ain't real sure whether I am or not.

To someone who accused him of procrastinating: Well, you know, actually I was going to procrastinate, but I kept putting it off 'til it was too dang late.

To someone who accused him of being ambitious: Shoot, if I was ambitious, I wouldn't even be talking to you.

To the question "What would you like people to say about you after you're gone?": I'd like the men to say "he enjoyed life" and the women to say "he was great in bed."

To a short-tempered young woman: Honey, if you want to become a sweet old lady, you've got to start out as a sweet young lady.

To the question, "'You finished?'": No, I'm Norwegian.

To someone who was displaying their knowledge of vintage wines: Wines are like women: I don't pretend to understand them; I just enjoy them.

To a host's question, "What do you drink?": Just about anything that's not locked up.

G. E. Kruckeberg

RESPONSIBILITY

"A man's first responsibility is to improve the human condition. That means being a good husband, a good father, a good citizen, and sometimes a good soldier. It means doing the best you can at whatever job you are given with whatever tools you have got. And it especially means looking out for others. We are all in the business of being human together, and whenever any man fails, we all lose a little."

Those words were written in my Daddy's cramped handwriting on the front flyleaf of a prayer book that somehow got tucked into my baggage the last weekend I was home before leaving for Korea in 1954. I never told him what those words meant to me during the long months of cold and boredom and doubt and fear, and he never asked. But I knew when I came across that book at the Demarcation Center in San Diego that it was very important to him that I understand what he had written. Daddy was not in the habit of writing about such things, and if he had sculpted it in neon lights it could not have made a greater impression on me.

To my Daddy, responsibility was the philosopher's stone, and it gave the man who possessed it freedom and maturity and honesty and, especially, manhood. He considered responsibility to be the one characteristic that unerringly differentiated the man from the boy, and he made it quite clear to me as I was growing up that what he expected me to be was a man.

Of course, not everything Daddy had to say about responsibility was pedagogic.

There aren't but two things in this world a man can count on: himself and his fingers.

Responsibility is a mental disease that men catch from women.

A man's major responsibility is taking it.

Responsible used to mean not making mistakes; nowadays it means being able to pay for your mistakes.

Responsibility is the seed of civilization.

Authority is reliability spelled frontwards.

Responsibility isn't staying out of trouble so much as it is staying out of other folks' troubles.

Give me reasons – excuses I can make myself.

If you want something done right, you gotta do it when you're sober.

A man is born irresponsible and honest. Responsibility is mostly a matter of learning to lie.

Responsibility is doing something you know you oughta do but don't want to.

Responsibility is often based on the fear of success.

Responsibility is a good cover for incompetence.

It's been my experience that most people are responsible – they're just responsible for different screwups.

Most folks'll take anything that's free except responsibility and good advice.

About the only thing that most folks are willing to give freely to others is responsibility.

The father of responsibility is ambition.

Taking on extra responsibility is one way of getting ahead – ache.

A man's first responsibility is always to himself.

Everybody is responsible – the question is for what.

Snakes and responsibility are two things you can leave lying around without fear that somebody's gonna take 'em.

I wouldn't mind being responsible if folks didn't start expecting you to act that way all the time.

Responsibility can be a big obstacle to success. A man can't get ahead if he's got to take everybody else along with him.

Silence breeds consent.

A man's first responsibilities are to those who are depending on him: his bookie, his bartender, wife, kids...

The major difference between the Japanese and Americans is that the Japanese believe in individual responsibility and group authority, while Americans believe in individual authority and group responsibility.

Responsible people respond.

I got the right to swing my arm anywhere I want – and you got the right to stick your nose in front of it all you want to.

You never know what kind of a man you're dealing with until you see him handle a horse – or a woman.

Responsibility is what a man's got to take when he can't find anybody else to blame.

Ours not to reason why. Ours but to figure out how.

If time flies, you're just not busy enough.

If responsibility is evil, it dang sure is a *necessary* evil.

Responsibility is what responsible people expect and irresponsible people demand.

The question isn't so much who was responsible as it is who was *ir*responsible.

Responsibility sometimes means taking the blame for somebody else's mistakes.

The only person in the world you can blame for your unhappiness is you.

People that have a lot of responsibility are always lazy people, because it's a lot easier to take responsibility than it is to give it.

Anybody can take responsibility, but only a masochist would keep it.

Accountability is a cheap substitute for responsibility.

Responsibility is mostly looking for what's right, and accountability is looking for what's wrong.

Accountability is paying your debts; responsibility is paying them on time.

Responsibility is a personal contribution; accountability is a personal imposition.

The trouble with accountability is it always stops somewhere.

THE SECOND AMENDMENT

My first gun was a Belgian made .22 single shot bolt action rifle. It was stocked for a boy of nine, and it had been new when my great grandfather gave it to my father on his ninth birthday. When Daddy gave it to me in the Spring of my ninth summer, the bluing was worn off and the extractor spring was broken. But to my young eyes, it was the most beautiful thing I had ever seen. I cleaned it incessantly, and although I was allowed to shoot only birdshot in it, I was responsible for the demise of more than a few blackbirds that had the audacity to invade Daddy's corn patch.

When I was eleven, I got my first shotgun, a single shot break action twenty gauge, and for the first time in my life I was in the position of being able to put food on the family table. But by then I knew that that was not the only reason for having a gun. I had been taught in school that the second article of the Bill of Rights was added to the Constitution at the insistence of those colonies who did not trust a federal government and demanded the means of protecting themselves from the anticipated and historically demonstrable excesses of such an institution.

Daddy, it seems, had no views at all on gun control during most of his life, but that was undoubtedly due to the fact that during most of his life the access to firearms had been totally unrestricted. It wasn't until after the assassination of John Kennedy, when the anti-gun kooks started to come out of the woodwork, that Daddy commented on the subject, and most of what follows is from that unfortunate era.

Daddy is gone now, but I know that if he were here, he would be in the forefront of the attack on current attempts to curtail our basic rights, and he would long, as I do, for a return to that seemingly far off and simpler time of freedom and responsibility and justice.

The Second Amendment is the first right.

The most basic human right is the right of a man to protect himself.

The Second Amendment wasn't put there so we could protect ourselves from criminals; it was put there so we could protect ourselves from the army.

As long as the government has guns, we need guns.

If the government thinks it's charitable to restrict guns, let their charity begin at home.

The folks that are against Saturday night specials are mostly Sunday morning hypocrites.

Trying to control crime by banning guns is like trying to control pornography by banning cameras.

Gun control won't stop crime. It'll create brand new ones, just like prohibition did.

The first thing Hitler did in '38 was take all the .38s away from the people.

I never saw a proposition for gun control that I couldn't shoot holes in.

Crime was here a long time before guns.

Guns have killed a helluva lot more bad people than good people.

Judges are responsible for more crime than guns ever were – so why don't we outlaw judges?

You can kill a man with a club or a knife – a gun just makes it easier to protect yourself from people that want to club you or knife you.

Everybody knows that newspapers lie, but nobody's suggesting we outlaw newspapers.

Gun control oughta be applied only to members of parole boards who turn killers loose – so law-abiding citizens could shoot them with impunity.

Criminals make crime; guns make good sense.

A gun is just a mindless tool; it's the mindless *fools* we've got to do something about.

Don't call a pistol a handgun. Handgun is Washingtonese for a kind of gun that folks don't really need.

SELFISHNESS

My cousin Donna had a new bicycle – a "two wheeler" as we used to call them. It was a full sized, twenty-six inch beauty, painted bright blue with white pin striping, and it had a little bell on the handlebar that you could ring in case someone got in your way. The fact that it was a girl's bike in no way deterred me from begging her to let me ride it, particularly since I was at the age when my legs were too short to reach the pedals of a full sized boys's bicycle and I could ride a girl's bicycle standing up.

Now my cousin Donna was at the time an only child, and the apple of my uncle Don's eye. The concept of sharing had either never been presented to her or had failed to make any impression whatsoever on her young mind. In a word, she was what we used to call "stingy," and it was, therefore, only after incessant and demeaning cajoling that I finally managed to wrangle from her one pitiful little ride around the block.

I can still remember that ride – the feel of the wind in my hair, the whisper of twenty-six inch B. F. Goodrich tires on the asphalt, the feeling of power when I accelerated, and the sudden determination as I rounded the last corner to make this ride last forever. Donna stepped out into the street when she saw me coming, apparently expecting me to honor our agreement that I was to have only one ride around the block. I threw every ounce of my forty-two pounds into pumping those pedals and rang the bell wildly, as Donna's mouth dropped open and she jumped back to the curb.

On my second turn around the block, Donna was jumping up and down with rage; on the third she was crying; and on the fourth, my Daddy was standing there beside her.

I took my licking like a man, but I felt obliged afterwards to try to explain my actions. "I wouldn't have done it," I lied, "if she wasn't so stingy."

Daddy looked me straight in the eye and said, "Boy, a person's entitled to be stingy with something of theirs, but not with something that belongs to somebody else."

Selfishness is the basis of survival.

A man's not measured by how happy he makes himself but by how happy he makes other folks.

A man that's not selfish isn't to be trusted.

I wouldn't give you a nickel for a man that didn't think enough of himself to be a little selfish.

Selfishness is just generosity confined to yourself.

You can be selfish all you want, as long as you're not selfish with something of mine.

Selfishness is social suicide.

Selfishness isn't a matter of caring too much for yourself but of not caring enough for others.

Generosity is selfishness that happens to benefit somebody else.

The only person it's easy to forgive selfishness in is yourself.

The only thing that makes most selfish people respectable is that they are also wealthy people.

The source of all freedom is selfishness.

"Enlightened" self-interest usually means "my" self-interest.

Nobody ever really believes an unselfish man.

Unselfishness is almost always based on selfishness.

Unselfish people are boring. The only thing that makes a man interesting is his love of himself.

Selfish people are usually lonely people.

Civility is 1% caring and 110% pretending to.

The difference between selfish and egotistical is the difference between drinking a beer and getting drunk.

All animals are selfish. Unselfishness is something that women invented to make it easier for them to civilize men.

A man tends to lose his perspective when he's in love – especially if he's in love with himself.

Selfishness is existentialism in action.

The greatest enemy of selfishness is ambition.

Wisdom begins where selfishness ends.

Vanity is the price of success.

SUCCESS

Daddy was very proud of the fact that I had achieved a Bachelor of Science degree from one of the most prestigious engineering schools in the world.   But I had graduated during the heady, post-sputnik years, when young engineers made their living following government contracts, and Daddy was appalled that on the eighth anniversary of my graduation, I was in my third job with my third company.

Daddy had retired from the same company that had hired him back when the country had started its slow climb out of the Depression, and I think he saw me as something of a butterfly. When I told him that I'd been laid off yet again and was moving 250 miles away to take a job with yet another company, his response was, "Why can't you just stay with the company you're with now?"

At the time, I'm not sure I understood the mechanics driving the system any better than he did, and my response was a simple, "Dad, I just can't."

"Don't ever say 'I can't'," he said. "Say 'I don't want to.' It's more honest and it gives you a better insight into why you never succeed."

In spite of Daddy's lack of insight into the effects of the cold war on technological employment opportunities, he did seem to have a pretty good handle on the meaning and mechanics of success in general, as is evidenced by the following.

Success is getting what you want, not what everybody else has got.

Succeeding may not be the most important thing in the world, but it sure beats the hell out of failing.

A man is successful when he makes more money than his wife can spend.

There are no great people – just great deeds.

Success in anything depends on a sort of myopia that insists on seeing opportunities where other folks see only problems.

You can't succeed at something you don't do.

The only reason for failure is believing it can't be done.

Succeeding comes from wanting to.

Persistence is the glue of success.

The secret to success is to never tell folks what they don't want to hear.

If you're still alive, you've been successful so far.

History always gets written by the winners.

Everybody wants success – until they get it.

Success is getting what you want; happiness is wanting what you get.

The fruits of success are most often disappointment and disillusion.

A man can't succeed if he's not trying to.

Success is not having any regrets.

Everybody wants to share your victories, but you've got to enjoy your defeats all by yourself.

Dumb luck is at least half of what a man needs to succeed at anything.

The easiest thing to succeed at is something that you like to do.

One thing that's easy to succeed at is minding your own business – mainly because you usually got a whole lot of help.

Failure is always a prerequisite to success.

Failure is the mark of creativity.

A man's got to do more than just work hard to succeed – he's got to know at what to.

The secret to success is training folks not to expect too much from you.

It's always easier for a man to hide his successes than it is to hide his mistakes.

Trying too hard can keep a man from getting what he wants almost as quick as not trying hard enough.

The first thing you gotta do to be successful is to look successful.

Success is feeling good about yourself.

The road to success is paved with good inventions.

A dilemma is a sort of mental block that keeps a man from seeing that he's always got more than two choices.

Find something you like to do that people will pay you for doing and you'll never have to work a day in your life.

The problem with success is a man doesn't learn anything from it.

If you're gonna brag, brag about where you are, not about where you been.

Difficulty is a losers word for opportunity.

If at first you don't succeed, blame it on somebody else.

If you want to succeed at what's important, learn to think like a woman.

Resting on your laurels will turn them into hemlock.

The difference between a success and a failure is the difference between a good actor and a bad actor.

Succeeding is like lying: the more you do it, the easier it gets.

The secret to success is never try to do more than you can do well.

VERBOSITY

Howard Grissom, a young man who lived down the road from us, stopped by late one summer afternoon to see my Daddy. The two men went out in the back yard and talked and drank beer and watched the sun go down behind the tree line back along the creek.

I was a senior in high school at the time, and old enough to listen to, if not to participate in, adult conversations – not that this one was all that exciting. Except for Howard's off-hand comment that he'd gotten notice of his induction into the army that morning, the talk revolved around the weather and war and politics and women and cars. When the mosquitoes got too bad, Howard went back home and Daddy and I went on into the house.

"What did Howard want?" Mama asked when she heard the screen door slam.

"He wants me to look after his family and his place while he's in Korea," Daddy said.

"I never heard him say anything like that," I argued. "He talked about dang near everything else, but he didn't even mention his family."

"When you get older," Daddy said, "you'll find that the things a man *doesn't* talk about are the things he's most concerned about."

Daddy generally lived by what he said, and the mere fact that I've managed to scavenge from the recesses of my memory a modest number of the things he had to say on the subject of verbosity is a pretty good indication that it wasn't one of his greater concerns.

The less you say the more you learn.

When a man is talking, he's taking up his time with something he already knows.

The true sign of elegance is knowing when to shut up.

Most folks are damaged more by what they say than by what's said about them.

If you can't keep your mouth shut, at least keep it empty.

A wise man learns to listen while he's talking.

A man's intelligence is measured not by how much he knows but by how much he's willing to tell.

A wise man talks only to teach and listens only to learn.

Man in the only animal whose ears close up when his mouth is open.

The less you say, the more folks listen.

The Socratic method is very effective – at getting people so ticked off they'll feed you hemlock just to shut you up.

'Fellow that talks to himself is usually more efficient than the fellow that goes around talking to everybody.

Talk is cheap – it's listening to it that'll cost you.

Don't speak unless you've got something to say.

Don't talk with your mouth full – or your head empty.

Ask and ye shall be questioned.

Speak when you're spoken to, and listen when you're being listened to.

A man that'll tell you everything he knows usually doesn't take long to do it.

A man will talk to anybody, and a woman will talk about anybody.

Engineers are the most honest people in the world. They'll tell you everything they know – and more.

'Fellow that says everything he's thinking isn't.

'Fellow that talks too much is generally scared of something.

My Daddy used to say that children should be seen and not heard, but after taking a good look at some of them, I think we might all be better served if they were heard and not seen.

It's been my experience that a man that talks a lot doesn't do a lot.

The more information you give folks, the more they feel they have got to do something with it.

A man can't spend without money, but he can talk without knowledge.

A man's mouth is like his purse: the more he opens it, the less he's got in it.

Communication is twenty percent talking and eighty percent listening.

The reason talk is cheap is that the supply exceeds the demand.

WEALTH

It was warm and cozy in the cab of Daddy's old truck. The sun that a few hours before had painted the oily-black water first purple then pink then orange, was now a blazing golden orb in the sky, and the warmth of its rays, captured by the dirt on the windshield, made one forget the earlier experience of predawn cold – if not the experience of having hauled in the seven bass that now resided in the ice chest in the back of the truck.

My brother was dozing, lulled by the warmth and the drone of the engine and the gentle rocking motion as Daddy picked our way up the old log road from the lake. As for myself, having imbibed an inordinate amount of the steaming, leather-colored brew from Daddy's big thermos, I was not only wide awake but in a somewhat contentious mood.

"Y'know, Daddy," I was saying, "you're a really smart man, and if you was to really put your mind to it, you could make a lot of money." At the time, I meant it as a compliment, although in later years I realized that it must have sounded more like a complaint.

"Well," Daddy said, "you might be right. But if I was to do that, I wouldn't have near as much time to take you fishing, now would I?"

There are two kinds of intelligent people: honest and rich.

Wealth may not be the most important thing in the world, but it's right up there with sex and baseball.

When I was a kid, I always wanted to be rich. Now that I'm older, I realize that I was.

Money is the proof of all evil.

The wages of sin is wealth.

Rich folks got that way from being more interested in money than in the things that money can buy.

Prosperity is the only thing standing in the way of progress.

Borrowing dulls the dread of usury.

Money is worth whatever you can buy with it.

Money is good for paying lawyers to see that you make more money so you can pay lawyers more.

All a man really needs is health, wealth, and everything else.

Wealth is like a cat: you don't own it – it owns you.

Money was made to be spent – but its greatest value comes from the expectation of spending it.

The great American dream is not to be rich – it's to *get* rich.

Everybody's poor; it's just that some folks have to spend more to stay that way.

You've got to be born either rich or smart.

Money doesn't make a man rich – it just makes him real busy.

Inherited wealth is the curse of human society.

Wealth makes more bums than poverty ever thought of making.

Class will tell – usually on itself.

America is the only country in the world where wealth takes the place of nobility.

Money's like sex: you never get enough of it, but the less you do get, the more you think about it.

Wanting comes from not having.

It's the lack of money, not the love of it, that's the root of all evil.

The more money you got, the more chance you got of somebody trying to take it away from you.

The rich worry a whole lot more about their wealth than the poor do about their poverty.

Money's a poor servant but it's one heck of a taskmaster.

Wealth and freedom don't mix well.

The main difference between rich folks and poor folks is that poor folks can tell who their friends are.

Manufacturing is the only source of wealth.

Wealth enables a man to buy more expensive reasons for not doing what he really wants to do.

Wealth is a poor substitute for intelligence.

Being rich is easier to prove than being right.

The only instrument that requires neither skill nor intelligence to play is the stock market.

They say Keynes played the stock market, and I reckon in order to play, a man has got to be about as ignorant of basic economic principles as he was.

A sure way to make a small fortune in the stock market is to start out with a big fortune.

The only difference between Wall Street and Las Vegas is that in Las Vegas they give you a drink on the house after they take your money.

Playing the stock market can't be gambling, because all of the gamblers I ever knew were too dang smart to get into stocks.

The only thing money's good for is to make somebody else happy.

The most profitable investment you can make is kindness.

The haves and the have-nots are usually the sons and daughters of the dids and the did-nots.

WOMEN

My Daddy was a great observer and an avid admirer of women of all ages, but he was particularly solicitous of older women. "Old ladies," he used to say, "are so used to being ignored that it doesn't take too much to please them." When I was growing up, I always thought that this proclivity was induced more by kindness than by anything else, but as I got older, I began to suspect that Daddy really *liked* old women. This idea was so incomprehensible to a boy in his early teens that I ventured to ask Daddy about it.

"Well," he said, "women seem to get better with age. Time has about the same effect on a man that wind and rain do on an outcropping; the softer parts wash away until only the hard granite core remains. Women, on the other hand, age like wine; the harsher parts settle out 'til all that's left is the sweet, clear elixir of femininity."

That sentiment is typical of my Daddy's feelings about women, and although his attentions were never overt, he was fond of observing and commenting on them, mostly outside of Mama's cognizance. Now that Mama's gone, however, I suppose it would do no harm to reproduce a few of those comments.

When you get right down to it, there aren't but two kinds of people in the world: men and women.

Women are the only civilizing influence in the world, and they always have been.

225

You can't ever keep a woman happy, but it sure as hell is fun trying.

I never met a woman I didn't like.

The Trojan War's the only war I ever heard of that was fought over something important.

The proper study of mankind is womankind.

It's probably a good thing that men don't understand women, 'cause women understand 'em and they don't like 'em.

Women can be confusing, exasperating, and infuriating, but they will never be: boring.

Hell hath no fury like a woman bored.

The only way to keep a woman is satisfied.

The reason men are never satisfied is that in order for a man to be satisfied, he's got to have a satisfied woman.

Never expect a lady to do the gentlemanly thing.

After God created man, He saw that he was going to be more than a match for the devil. So He created woman to sort of even things up a bit.

A good woman's like a carnival mirror: she makes a man look twice as big as he really is.

A woman can bring out the best in a man – even when it's not there.

When women try to let on that they are more virtuous than men, the only people that they're fooling is men.

There's no such thing as an ugly woman; it's just that some of them are prettier than others.

A woman's the only creature in the world that can hold a fifteen-minute conversation with somebody's answering machine.

Poets have been saying for centuries that women are prettier than men. 'Course all them poets were men.

Women ought to be prettier than men – they spend a helluva lot more time and money at it.

Women are nothing but trouble, and I been in trouble all my life.

The mass of women lead lives of diet aspiration.

The only thing more dangerous than a woman is a Christian, and the only thing more dangerous that a Christian is a Christian woman.

A woman in love is like a runaway diesel: the more you try to throttle her down, the faster she runs.

Women always try to make the best out of a bad situation; a man usually manages to make the worst out of a good one.

Women generally know less than men, but they understand a hell of a lot more.

Changing one's mind is not the exclusive prerogative of women – it just takes men longer.

Men are more organized than women – because their mothers trained them to be.

Women like to be taken care of almost as much as men like taking care of them.

Behind every successful man there's a bunch of women.

Men put junk in the attic; women have a garage sale and get paid to let somebody else's husband put it in *their* attic.

If you can just keep the women happy, everything else will take care of itself.

The reason we call them the opposite sex is that no matter what you tell them to do, they will invariably do the opposite.

The only way to make a woman obey you is to tell her to do what she has already done.

If you can please a woman 50% of the time, you're normal; if you can please one 75% of the time, you're a genius; and if you can please one 100% of the time, look out – she's after something.

There's only one kind of man that'll argue with a woman: a loser.

There are as many different worlds as there are different women, and half as many heavens as there are women's arms.

All men may be created equal, but no man is created equal to a woman.

Women are like cats: if you pet two of them at the same time, they both get ticked off.

Hell hath no furry like the mother of a woman scorned.

Men are still boys, but girls are already women.

Men like to think that all men are created equal; women are glad they're not.

It's a dang good thing that women are beautiful, 'cause they sure couldn't survive on civility.

Men play politics; women work it.

The more a woman pays for a hair cut the more she looks like she needs one.

It takes a woman a long time to get used to something, but as soon as she does, she's tired of it.

A woman always has the last word in an argument. Anything a man says after that is the start of a new argument.

The way to keep a woman happy is to make sure she always comes first.

A good woman is one who can get a man who's down and out up and in.

Women are more reliable than men; they can always be relied upon to be unpredictable.

Always respond to a woman when she's sexy, but never respond when she's angry.

Man proposes but woman imposes.

WORRY

Throughout most of its twelve hundred year history, the word "worry" has been a transitive verb. The cat worries the mouse or the student worries the teacher. It has been only quite recently that the word has become intransitive.

This etymological evolution seems to have followed an increasing tendency for modern people to "worry themselves" – a tendency that has become so prevalent that the second word in the phrase, being deemed unnecessary, has been dropped. But whether we worry transitively or intransitively, the consequences are the same. It has been suggested that stress and tension and high blood pressure are products not so much of twentieth century life as of the self-worrying of twentieth century people.

Daddy used to say it a bit differently. "Worrying," he always said, "won't do you any good – unless your intention is to make yourself sick."

Only a damn fool worries about something he can't change, and only a lazy man worries about something he can.

If it's going to worry you, don't do it; and if you're going to do it, don't worry about it.

The secret to poor health is worry.

It's 'most always the stuff you *don't* worry about that bites you in the butt.

Problems are like opinions: yours may be unusual, but you're not the only one that's got them.

The reason a lot of folks never have any joy is because they worry it to death.

Some folks seem to be more scared of living than they are of dying.

There are no little problems – unless they're somebody else's.

A man can't take the time to worry about the past when the future's bearing down on him at sixty minutes an hour.

It's too late to worry about the past and too early to worry about the future.

Worriers have got to worry. If you fix it so they don't have to worry themselves about food and medical care, they will worry other folks about whales and minks.

If you spend all your time worrying about what could happen, it will.

What you foresee is what you get.

Worrying is the first sign of senility and the last sign of immaturity.

The thing I like about worrying is that it's one of the few things a man can put off with impunity.

Worry is the major cause of most major causes.

Worrying is a lot like lying: the more you do it, the more you've got to.

It's easier to worry if you don't know what you're doing.

Worry is caused mostly by not having enough to do.

What a man worries about becoming is generally what he already is.

There are dang few atheists in foxholes – and even fewer Christians out of 'em.

ABOUT THE AUTHOR

G. E. Kruckeberg was born in Fort Wayne, Indiana and, after having served for four years in the U. S. Navy, he earned a Bachelor's Degree in Engineering from Purdue University. He has lived for two years in Korea and for six years in Tokyo, Japan, where he studied at Sophia University. He currently lives in Houston, Texas with his wife, Ann, who is a writer of mystery fiction, and their three cats, Shere Khan, Misha, and Mardi Gras. *Things My Daddy Used To Say* was inspired by the Kruckeberg's three sons, Edward, Mark, and John, and was written to pass along to them, and to posterity, the wisdom of their paternal grandfather.

Printed in the United States
125693LV00003B/205-231/A

9 781410 798138